Behind the Iron Curtain
Tears in the Perfect Hockey "GULAG"

by

Maxim Starchenko

RoseDog✿Books

PITTSBURGH, PENNSYLVANIA 15222

RoseDog Books
701 Smithfield Street
Pittsburgh, PA 15222
Visit our website at *www.rosedogbookstore.com*

ISBN: 978-1-4349-8553-8
eISBN: 978-1-4349-7548-5

Foreword
By Walter Babiy

When Maxim asked me to write a foreword for his narrative, I had to revisit that well of emotion experienced during my bittersweet encounter with the fabled team from Kharkiv, Ukraine— "Druzhba-78."

During the past seven decades, I have played in many countries as a hockey nomad and as an ambassador. I have skated on the marshland ponds of Canada, played shinny with the street boys on the flooded city square in Helsinki, quaffed beer with the Bohemian glass blowers, played on the rinks of Luzniki's Palace of Sport, and many arenas of North America, with the "greats" of bygone years.

Looking back, I came away with lifelong friends and extraordinary experiences, but none of those nostalgic and astonishing moments prepared me for what I found behind the illusion and sordid secrets of a perfect hockey team.

They were the dream team and the best Bantams in the world. They were the Globetrotters on steel and we all believed in their artistry and magic. Indeed, when this hockey team from Kharkiv, Ukraine, burst on the international scene, it was to herald a new beginning of hope, vision, and exhalation; yes, I saw the legendary phoenix in the amazing boys of "Druzhba-78" and the rebirth of their nation.

Sadly, this nation's lament "Cry not for me Ukraine" are the voices of millions who perished from hunger, wars, and oppression; their national anthem, "Sche Ne Vmerla Ukraina," haunts us that this country still lives and has not yet died.

Would these prophetic words be the inspiration to break the bonds of their nation's legacy of tragedy and pain?

In Kharkiv, I saw children play as children do, singing nursery songs while spinning on a wobbly carousel; while these young lads, their youth forsaken, chose the calling of a Machiavellian despot and his cauldron of despair. Once there, they could only murmur and obey.

In a flight of fantasy, little did the boys of "Druzhba-78" realize that fear and evil would be their constant companion and their hockey dreams all but shattered and crushed by tears, tyranny, and greed.

Did this happen to other treasures of the state? The likes of gymnast Olga Corbet of Russia, Nadia Comaneci of Romania, or figure skater Oksana Baiul of Ukraine, perhaps, as they too must have their horror stories in healing their broken bodies and minds.

To understand one only has to read Solzhenitsyn's *The Gulag Archipelago*,[1] The text on Beria,[2] and the volumes on the Stalin[3] purges to realize how that communist system would spawn an acerbic mentor in charge of the boys of "Druzhba-78."

1. Solzhenitsyn A., *The Gulag Archipelago: An Experiment in Literary Investigation*. (New York, New York: Harper & Row Publishers, Inc., 1973)
2. Dictator—Stalin's notorious police chief.
3. Supreme ruler of the Soviet Union 1929–1953.

The Author's Note

Before my reader begins the story ahead, some explanation is necessary. The magnitude of events described in the following chapters raises many moral questions. I gave a detailed account of major circumstances and daily undertakings within the realm of the hockey team Druzhba-78, but I only touched upon my personal psychological consequences. I decided to leave that to my reader's interpretation, as one must come to his/her own conclusion about the severity of the events. I briefly provide my opinion, but in no way do I expect all to view the circumstances with the same judgment. I also included only a small portion of the atrocities our coach, Ivan Pravilov, unleashed upon his players. His mind games, his constant insults and harassment (mental and physical), and his abuse happened far more often than the story describes. It was normal for him to randomly pick a player and harass him throughout the day or the entire hockey trip. The trips were frequent, to the point that I probably spent only a third of my childhood with my family.

The story mentions my parents, and their role is of great importance. The tone could mislead you to believe I eventually lost my love and compassion for them. So, going back to the much needed explanation, I first and foremost want to clarify my relationship with them. I love them dearly. I laugh with them and share every bit of my post-Druzhba life. Although they saw the symptoms during my ten years on Druzhba-78, they only recently learned the details of what happened, as I kept everything to myself. During my recent trip home, I raised the topic of Ivan's cruelty and began with a few stories, to which my parents sat quietly not believing their ears. My father left the room after a couple of them, saying he had enough. My mother was dumbfounded, not understanding how Pravilov was able to mislead them and make fools out of them. She asked me why I never told them about it then, but I could only reply that such things were not easy to discuss or talk about. Ivan's strict approach attracted my parents, because they thought his disciplinarian methods benefited their son. I wish they had known the degree his wicked and sadistic mind was capable of reaching. Seeing my parents' reaction, I can only imagine Ivan's fate had they known the truth when I was still a child. Perhaps the long delay in delivering such news was a benefit to my family. I was able to calm them down and explain that my life was in good shape. I had met great friends who gave me unconditional love and support, and worrying about the dark past would be a nuisance. I feel and understand my parents' love, and for that reason only recently made an attempt to resurface this gruesome story.

You will read about my feelings and thoughts as they appeared then, but these should not be judged as my current state of mind. They were only a mere reflection of my childhood, but in no way of my adulthood. Love and peace make up my everyday life now.

During and after your reading, you might be compelled to believe I continue to hold a grudge against my former teammates from Druzhba-78. You will encounter instances which could lead anyone to the utmost hatred toward one's adversaries. You might be emotionally drawn against those who unquestionably followed Ivan's commands and abused and humiliated their own teammates. But I and each of my former teammates know that every one of us at one point or another is guilty of that charge, at least of being resentful and reproachful. Are we all expected to hate and despise each other and disregard the fact that Ivan Pravilov intentionally imposed such feelings and thoughts upon us? We were very young and naïve, and from the get-go, our beloved coach used it against us to empower himself and rule without hindrance. He separated us, creating the environment of complete resentment and distrust in each other. And, therefore, I do not hold a grudge against my former teammates, but I ask for their forgiveness for ever having such feelings and allowing my mind to be corrupted by the vicious tyrant. My only hope is that they feel the same toward me.

I also feel I should explain the chosen title of this book *Behind the Iron Curtain: Tears in the Perfect Hockey GULAG*. The story of Druzhba-78 revolves around a secretive and brutal environment that Ivan created and in which he continuously abused his players, calling them "his children." He encouraged us to inform on each other. Thus, we could not trust each other and were cautious about every word we spoke. Our behavior was robotic to the point of us not making a sound or a move without his permission. We were brainwashed into believing that he was our savior, and our parents were our nemeses. He was to be considered the standard of moral expectations.

In comparison, the Soviet regime where our team took its roots was based on fear, persecution, extermination, and utmost secrecy, reminiscent of Ivan Pravilov's methods and philosophies; hence, the first part of the title *Behind the Iron Curtain*. Many of you are familiar with the term from the Cold War years. Stalin's iron hand would not allow any anti-Soviet propaganda in or out of the country. Those who tried simply ended up shot or sent to Soviet concentration camps for slave labor, where millions disappeared in their midst. Likewise on Druzhba, no anti-Ivan propaganda was tolerated, and the culprits were punished severely. As today's renowned hypocrite, Stalin always portrayed himself to outsiders to be the savior of the people, and did it very well. However, his true story would totally contradict popular opinion. Our coach's case would not be any different. In the Soviet Union, *comrade* was the word applied to each citizen to represent comradeship among all, but it was only a word and no more. With this in mind, each player on Druzhba-78 was supposed to be *Droog* (friend), in relation to the title *Druzhba* (friendship), but after Ivan's countless mind games and its repercussions, the team's name was only a word and no more.

The *GULAG* part comes with the environment that Pravilov created within the team. GULAG was a long chain of Soviet concentration camps that stood for *Gosudarstvennoe Upravlenie Lagerey* (State Administration of Camps). It was a system of informers and spies that made most distrustful of each other. Inmates became robotic puppets and executioners. Some aggressively pursued their motives, while others passively awaited their fate and hoped for the best. Similar situations took place under Ivan's reign. Some aggressively applied Ivan's decrees against certain teammates, while others passively held them in contempt. Much of it was subtle and inconspicuous to an outsider, but not to the insider. GULAGs were designed to correct the minds of nonconformists through slave labor, just like Ivan, I believe, eventually used us to build his name and program. When a player no longer served a purpose in his mind, Pravilov threw him out and left him to fend for himself. In the GULAG system, many of those arrested were shot almost immediately as incorrigible elements in the communist society; I believe Ivan would not have hesitated to do the same if given the chance. After all, he used to remind us on many occasions that we would behave differently if machine guns stood in every corner of the building.

Some of my former teammates might disagree with me on the extreme comparison. How could I relate Stalin's system of annihilation to Ivan's regime within Druzhba-78? Let's look at one of the examples. Solzhenitsyn gave us something to ponder with his *The Gulag Archipelago: An Experiment in Literary Investigation* (1973). Several of the interrogation methods upon the civilians described in his book resemble Pravilov's punishment methods. For example, people were denied sleep throughout the night, forced to stand still in a brightly lit room. If they moved even an inch, beatings would ensue. I had a similar experience under Ivan more than once. There were good cop-bad cop impersonations that interrogators used interchangeably, which Ivan performed brilliantly without a second person. Many were also forced into becoming an informant and spy. Orlando Fige's *The Whisperers: Private Life in Stalin's Russia* (2007) mentions that "soviet citizens were encouraged to report on neighbors, colleagues, friends, and even relatives. Vigilance was the first duty of every Bolshevik." Likewise, we were encouraged in front of the entire team to inform Ivan about a certain player and ridicule him to add more salt to the wound. All who were interrogated had been asked to denounce their association with any other affiliation (be it true or not) and announce their love for their leader, Josef Stalin. In Ivan's case, I was constantly forced to say I loved my coach the most.

On a bigger scale, Stalin's paranoia of no trust to anyone resembled Ivan's frequent mind games that only created the environment of distrust and resentment toward and among his players. Ivan's inhumane brutality saw no end, and just like Stalin, he continued his ways until the end.

Ivan frequently referred to his players as "traitors," "fascists," and "Jews."* Traitors? In the Soviet Union, ordinary citizens would be shot, or at least brutally beaten and interrogated, for a mere comment about its government's poor performance. On Druzhba-78, Ivan constantly reminded us of our betrayal, never clarifying against whom and what, but severely punishing us as a result. Fascists? Ivan repeatedly placed us in this category, despite the fact that we were no more than ten years old. Jews? I do not understand why this term was used as an insult. Hitler exterminated nearly the entire population in Europe, and was not he a Nazi fascist? If Pravilov despises Jews, would not this make him a Nazi fascist? I would say so.

You might also be confused about how Druzhba's coach was able to impose his atrocities upon his players. Where were their parents? I believe this question may be the hardest to understand, but the truth lies in subtle cultural differences between the Western world and the Behind the Iron Curtain world. First, my parents saw me at the local rink only four times throughout my entire hockey career. They never traveled to see me play abroad, and my hockey life was my own. They were busy with their daily lives and only focused on my academic performance. Such circumstances were a norm in that culture. The government provided an efficient urban transportation system, and there was no immediate need for owning a car (most people could not afford it). There was no need for constant parental supervision. Children traveled on their own, taking care of their daily problems and activities by themselves from an early age. In North America, on the other hand, owning a vehicle is a must for daily transportation. Such circumstances allow parents to constantly supervise their children and their activities. Therefore, coaches and instructors are under much greater scrutiny.

Second, many changes occurred in the Western world in the last several decades. Civil rights were enforced and such brutalities would not be tolerated. In the Soviet Union, on the other hand, laws existed against child abuse, but they were rarely enforced considering the fearful attitude of its citizens toward the oppressive regime of our authorities. Much was let go and disregarded. Ivan Pravilov quickly recognized this phenomenon and made it work in his own favor. He bullied and oppressed anyone resisting his methods, and got away with it without much opposition. Other coaches and authorities

---

* The term was used by Ivan Pravilov in a derogatory sense to portray an individual as greedy, cunning, selfish, etc. The author wishes to clarify that he does not support this stereotype.

knew of his sadistic methods but remained silent. Consequently, Pravilov ruled us virtually unchallenged and forced his subjects to succumb to his will.

Lastly, as far as I am aware of, all parents were ordinary working class citizens. None of them held high-ranking positions and were expected to quietly perform their job duties. They could neither object nor argue. Pravilov recognized that and, using a dictatorial approach, was able to oppress any disapproval. From the beginning, he also lured all parents with his enthusiasm into believing that their children were in good hands. But gradually, he distanced all players from their parents with constant brainwashing during after-practice meetings. "Anything that happens on this team stays on this team, and no one, not even a parent, should stick one's nose where it does not belong," he used to say. In no time, my parents could not tell me what to do or how to live, because the coach knows best.

Introduction

This is a story of my experiences on the infamous hockey team called Druzhba-78 from Kharkiv, Ukraine. In the mid-1990s, we traveled around the world and dazzled spectators with finesse and intensity. "Druzhba" means friend-ship, and 78 stood for the year all players on the squad were born. To many spectators, Druzhba-78 was a dream team that made its mark on the world hockey scene by winning numerous prestigious international tournaments. We shocked our opponents with skill, winning many games with double digits on the scoreboard. We made headlines in prestigious newspapers like the *Boston Globe* and the *Edmonton Journal*. We had, as many thought, a team of future Olympians. Some even dubbed Druzhba-78 a "Cinderella team" that came out of origins of the oppressive former Soviet Union and eventually became the shining moment in very young Ukrainian history. However, no one could see or expect that such greatness could come at a much higher cost.

This is a firsthand account of the great cost that every player on Druzhba-78 paid for the team's "greatness." My primary goal is to relieve myself of the huge emotional burden I carry on my shoulders whenever topics of child abuse and molestation arise. I still have periodic nightmares of all the horror I experienced at the hands of my coach, Ivan Pravilov. What we went through could never be fully understood and believed by an outsider. I also hope to encourage other players from Druzhba-78 to step forward and unite in an effort to let the world know that the "Cinderella" story about our team was not a fairy tale after all. Our fear of him could only be matched by the fear that people had during the Stalin years of the Soviet Union before, during, and after WWII. Under Stalin, innocent citizens would be shot or sent to GULAGs. Under Pravilov, we were punished by other means. Instead of being killed or sent to a concentration camp, we experienced repeated brutal physical and mental abuse perpetrated by our coach.

Wherever Ivan went, he portrayed himself as a genuine person. Many believed him and looked at him in awe. My parents initially saw him as a great role model for me. Other people were inspired by his enthusiasm and perseverance. But this was only a façade of his true identity. I learned about Ivan's "unique" methods of training and disciplining shortly after I started playing for him. His former players (he temporarily had a team of players born in 1975) asked me on several occasions if Ivan used to beat us. I would reply, "Of course not," simultaneously wondering how they could have known. At the time, I knew nothing about Ivan's previous team and took them as strangers who I would not trust with the truth. I am writing this book for many hockey officials and federations to take serious note of the incidents that occurred. I believe that no one who raises his/her hand against a child should be allowed under any circumstances to be near children; moreover, I hope the record will speak for itself and you will see that such a man does not deserve to walk free on this earth. What Ivan Pravilov did, and probably still continues to do, is inexcusable. Pravilov currently denies all allegations against him, but at the end of this book, I invite readers to draw their own conclusions.

Since my disassociation with Ivan, many have asked me, "Are the rumors of Ivan's abuse toward his players true?" I would always reply "yes," but knew that I could never fully express the depth and horror of what actually occurred to anyone who was not personally involved. Pravilov's former "Druzhba-78" website stated: "His (Ivan Pravilov's) approach also promotes sportsmanship, enables each student to more fully understand themselves in the process of developing sound moral and human qualities." I find this ironic, as Ivan was unable to demonstrate any sound moral or human qualities during the entire ten years I was under his authority. He preached to us about honesty and loyalty but was unable to demonstrate these same characteristics. Throughout the ten years I spent with Pravilov, the greedier and more untrustworthy he became. Several core players were literally thrown off the team without any hope for the future, despite Ivan's promise that no one would be kicked out without their own will. Several other players were assigned other roles ("assistant" coaches) by Ivan toward the end of our team's existence. He planned to collect a new generation of young hockey players and we would be his "assistants." In his opinion, his players were always ungrateful and not worthy of anything that was given to them. Pravilov became a master of manipulation and deceit.

Because Ivan was highly skilled at controlling his behaviors around outsiders, only few ever observed, or consequently challenged, the actions he took against his players. He was always careful about picking his victims and keeping others unaware of what was happening right under their own nose. Several years ago, Walter Babiy from Edmonton, Alberta, Canada, published a book called *Reign of Fear* about our team and our coach. Babiy was involved with the team on many levels, from facilitating our trips to Canada for various tournaments and exhibition games to billeting various players, and Ivan himself, during the trips. Several players provided input to his story, and I do not think Walter anticipated the severity of Ivan's abuse. He was shocked to find out that Ivan beat up players in his own house while he was staying there. People who have read the book were outraged that someone could be so cruel to children. Some even said he should be locked up in prison for his deeds. Pravilov's malevolence extended far beyond what Walter, an outside observer of our team, had documented. The stories in his book are only a little fraction of what the players actually endured with Ivan.

This is where my story comes in. I can no longer stand to look at articles that praise Ivan like he is a "hockey god." I cannot bear to hear people talk about his "high moral standards," when my experiences were the complete opposite. I cannot watch any more of Ivan's deceit and manipulation. I firmly believe that the time has come for this story to be told by someone who had firsthand experience and knowledge. I hope that my readers will not stop halfway, asking, "Is it possible?" as many will find these atrocities difficult to believe. Every player from the core group of Druzhba-78 knows the truth of what happened, but not everyone will step forward. We all have different perspectives on Ivan's motives and responsibilities for his abuse, and we are all at different points in our recovery. While a student at Wayne State University, I specifically took several psychology courses, hoping that I could more clearly understand Ivan's actions and what had driven him. In the end, no explanation could excuse his actions.

During the time of Druzhba-78, some stories did leak out. After minimal investigation, the International Ice Hockey Federation indicated they had no intention to pursue this matter, because there was no hard evidence. The topic of Ivan's cruel treatment of his players was forgotten. This matter should be of great importance to the hockey and sports community at large, and I truly hope that all of my former teammates will support my story and come forward with their own experiences. The incidents in this book are only those that I personally experienced or witnessed directly. I also saw the outcome of Ivan's abuse and humiliation toward other players, where incidents or punishments were executed behind closed doors, but many of these were too personal for me to discuss. I would rather have them told by the personally involved players themselves. After all is said and done, I consider myself lucky, being one of the least punished players on the team. In fact, several players were constantly singled out for abuse and harassment that significantly surpassed my personal experiences. The following story can really shock you, but it is only a small portion of a bigger picture. One could only imagine the magnitude of Pravilov's tyranny and vicious abuse.

I have no intention of forcing you to believe anything that is written here, but I would like you to really think if anyone would fabricate such an experience merely for the sake of publicity. Scanning through the Internet, I found the incident about a Canadian junior hockey coach, Graham James, sexually abusing some of his players. The story was told in greater detail in Laura Robinson's book *Crossing the Line* (1998). Chapter eight's title quoted

"Everybody in the league knew about it. Nobody did anything." It put the entire story in perspective, encompassing all that was wrong and overlooked. Such topics are very hard to speak about, as they bring many bad memories, and this is no easy task for me either. More than fourteen years have passed since I parted company with Ivan Pravilov, but the vision of each moment of humiliation and abuse stays in my mind like it happened days ago. I used to catch myself many times clenching my fists, while memories brought me back to those days. Sometimes I wonder what the next generation of players went through after our group split up. My gut tells me the picture is not pretty; I can only hope that, someday, this legacy will end.

Interestingly enough, Ivan's demeanor and attitude did give him an undesirable status in the world community. Browsing on the Internet, I found his name on the Interpol website, associated with charges against life and health. The situation forced me to dig deeper and research the causes for this charge. Apparently, there was a shooting incident in Kharkiv, Ukraine, and my former coach was involved in the case. He was not supposed to leave the country because of this case, but somehow, he ended up in the United States. I do wonder how he was able to sneak past Ukrainian authorities and pass through U.S. customs without incident.

Nonetheless, Ivan continued to make many believe in his righteousness. Newspapers like the *Boston Globe* raved about his "godly like genius" in developing hockey players. Many defend him because current and former players from Druzhba say he is innocent and "the best coach out there"—so typical of anyone under his reign. Several Americans and Canadians even send their own children to Ukraine for Ivan's training and provide positive feedback in regards to his methods. To some degree, I could understand their point of view. They saw no abuse and humiliation on Ivan's behalf. They did not witness Ivan's wrath upon his players. However, like any smart politician, his ability to conceal the madness showed thorough planning and manipulation. During my years on Druzhba, Ivan also invited a Canadian player to Ukraine who went to school with us and was involved in daily undertakings. But he was always left outside the closed doors when a serious issue arouse. He was not allowed to witness the true horror of Ivan's methods. He was kept in the dark just like anyone who Ivan considered an outsider.

Ivan Pravilov could never let the story get out. It would create an international scandal that our former coach could not afford to endure. The media could never find out about his true demeanor and how terrible he was to "his" children. This would undermine his plans for creating a hockey empire based on his *true* moral standards. He would have to face the International Ice Hockey Federation as well as the Ukrainian authorities, although I doubt that the latter would do much to investigate the problem. He would lose everything he strived for his entire life.

But the story must be told. The hockey world needs to know the truth about Ivan Pravilov. The time has come for his Iron Curtain to be torn down.

The Beginning

My first encounter with Ivan Pravilov came on September 2, 1986, when I was sitting in a classroom in school #103. During one of the lessons, he walked in and explained to the whole class that on September 9, there would be a soccer tournament after school among the second graders. He recorded the names of the students who would represent our class and left shortly after. After school, I raced home to tell the news to my parents and could not stop thinking about the upcoming event. The day came and after playing several games, for one reason or another, he picked me to come to one of his team's soccer practices, also explaining that I would play ice hockey in the winter. I was only eight years old and full of naïve expectations. *Oh boy*, I thought, *how exciting!* At that moment, my life had taken a path that I could not have imagined in my dreams and nightmares.

The first couple of months went by very quickly. I cherished every moment of my time during the practices and scrimmages. Ivan presented himself as a caring and responsible individual, the characteristics my parents and I appreciated very much. All was well, and it seemed to be a dream come true. However, after the initial couple of months, some abnormalities in Ivan's attitude toward his players began to surface. I began to notice that his patience was very short. He either could not control his emotions or purposefully used intimidation as a method of getting things done his way. When I could not perform a drill to his standards, I would receive a stare with bulging eyes and a hissing sound that was terrifying to me as a young child. Occasionally, he would smack me with a hockey stick in the back of my knees with a full swing, as a way to make me bend them lower. The force of the impact would shoot through my legs and the rest of the body. Sometimes, my legs became numb and lost any feeling. Every time that happened, I squeezed my teeth as hard as I could to avoid showing him that the pain affected me in any way. He would also provide a blow with a flat part of the hockey stick blade on the buttocks, and in those days, the protection there was minimal. This would not be a slight "go faster" blow that encouraged players. The impact would send shivers through my body and the stinging agony was unbearable. After one or two of those, my buttocks would always take on a dark purple color the next day, and sometimes, I received five to ten such hits at once. Ivan called it "stick massage."

In the summer of 1987, I experienced Ivan's first major rage against me. This situation had risen gradually over a long period of time, and Ivan seemed to have no more patience with my tendencies. In the spring that preceded the summer incident, I began jerking my head forward, extending my neck. I could not explain to my parents why I did so, but with time, I did it more frequently. They repeatedly asked me if I could remember anything out of the ordinary that happened to me, but I could not recall any incident. We also went to see a doctor who declared there was nothing wrong. However, the tendency persisted and became worse over a couple of months. Ivan began to threaten me that he would lay his stick on my neck if I continued in a similar manner. I did not fear his threats enough yet and continued the habit. During the summer break, my grandmother took me to a shaman, thinking that nothing else could fix the problem. Although I initially told her that the session helped, I still felt the same, and shortly after admitted there had been no progress. Upon my arrival to Kharkiv, the practices resumed and Ivan's verbal threats began to worsen. "Stop jerking your neck," he would say in a hissing and intimidating tone. In no time, he resorted to violence, and during one of the practices on the ice, he hit me several times on the back of my neck. Not wanting to receive another series of such blows, I began to focus greatly on my neck and reduced the jerking. However, the problem could not cease completely. My parents still noticed it occasionally but believed I was improving and needed no further treatment. Ivan, on the other hand, thought otherwise. One day, upon our team's entrance into the locker room to prepare for practice, Ivan stopped me and told me to approach him. Considering that I had no equipment on to protect me from any blows, I did not fear being hit and stepped forward. He instructed me to turn sideways and not to move. I did as I was told and the next second, Ivan swung a stick out from beside him, landing it across the back of my neck. The blow was agonizing, but I would not move and tried to withstand the abuse. A tear trickled down my cheek, but I stood still. The next moment, a second blow followed. Apparently, one time was not enough. This time, it landed on the back side of my shoulders and the damage was surprisingly minimal. "Will you stop your jerking now?" he asked, with his question sounding more like an order. I responded that I would try, which I learned was not satisfactory. My coach wanted a concrete answer of "yes." Thus, he swung his stick a couple of additional times to reinforce his point and landed it straight on my neck. He actually aimed his swings this time, allowing for more accurate hits.

My neck hurt badly, but considering the severity of Ivan's rage, I could not gather enough strength to ask him "why?" In my mind, arguing with a madman would be pointless and could provoke a harsher punishment. My father always reminded me in the past that if punished, I must be at some fault. So all I could do was take it and live with it, regardless if the reason was justified or not. I stood there motionless, accepting the blows and answering Ivan's questions "yes" and "no." After about seven or eight swings, the blows stopped and I was reminded verbally not to jerk my neck again. The day continued as usual and my parents never found out about the incident. The "treatment" had definitely improved my neck jerking, because I was extremely terrified of another such session and forced myself to remedy the situation. Later, my parents jokingly mentioned that my problem had faded away and thought of different reasons behind it. Understanding my father's ways and thinking that my mother would not really raise the issue, I simply let it be. In addition, being brought up with my father's mind-set, I actually felt somewhat proud of my accomplishment. I faced the problem, I did not complain, and I also came out stronger than before, or so I thought.

The second incident that significantly stood out in my mind happened during our trip to Leningrad (currently St. Petersburg) in the winter of 1987–88. The trip was intended to be pleasant, with us visiting many historical marvels of the city. But from the very beginning, Ivan decided to focus on my every move, which did not help me to feel comfortable and made things worse. The whole scenario began at one of the cafeterias where the team stopped for lunch. After filling my tray with food and setting it at a table, I noticed the utensils were missing and started walking back to get them. As I walked by the table at which Ivan was sitting, I was asked, "Why are you going back there?" When Ivan heard my reply, that I forgot the utensils, he commanded me to eat without them. Because the meal consisted of soup, mashed potatoes, and beef cutlets, I thought it could not be eaten without a spoon and a fork. So I assumed for a moment that Pravilov was joking and again moved to get the utensils. Ivan raised his voice and asked, "Are you bad?" As I turned around, he made a gesture with his hand for me to approach him. As soon as I did so, he began telling me that I lost my mind and for the rest of the trip should eat all my meals using my hands. I stood in front of him for about thirty seconds, trying to absorb the information and could not believe he was actually serious about it. *For crying out loud*, I thought to myself, *how absurd my coach sounds*. After a few moments, he asked me to leave his sight. I went back to my seat and began eating anything that I could with my hands. Although I was surprised at my coach's reaction and command, I also believed that it was my fault and this could be a good lesson not to forget again. So, I went along with it and continued eating my meals using only my hands. After two days of our visit, we began playing local teams, and my performance did not satisfy Ivan's standards. Instantly, Pravilov decided to teach me a lesson, although I still do not know what lesson that was, by making me sleep standing up.

The team stayed in a small hotel, with four players per room. On the third night, I was to wait for Ivan, awake in my room, standing up in the middle. My roommates shut the lights off, while I stood there trying to be awake. I began my post in the dark hoping Ivan would come in soon and let me go to sleep. After some time, I could not hold my position and began to lean back. There was a table behind me, so I sat down on the floor, leaning back against the edge. I tried to stay awake for some time, but in the end, my exhaustion overtook me. The next moment, I remember being woken up by a sudden light in the room. As I tried to recover my position and state of mind, Ivan rapidly walked toward me with a furious look on his face. He grabbed my shirt with one hand at my chest, lifted me up, and then without hesitation, swung his free fist into my face. When it connected with my jaw, it generated a clicking sound that woke me up quickly. Right then I became scared and started leaning back away from him. "Wake up," he said. "Who allowed you to sleep?" After several degrading comments by Ivan, the feeling of fright and confusion overwhelmed me. I could not understand his problem with me and why he would not let it go. Suddenly, he released his arms and said, "To be continued and do not fall asleep this time." On his way out of our room, he left the light on, making a clear statement of what was expected. The next time I saw him, I was lucky. Through my dozing state, I heard Pravilov's footsteps toward our door. By the time he opened it, I was standing straight. Remembering my recent encounter, I showed no signs of sleepiness. He began the barrage of name-calling and verbal assaults on each of my personal deficiencies. There seemed to be no end and it continued in this manner for another hour or so. In the end, he told me to go to bed and the lesson would continue another night. Waiting for Ivan's return each of the following nights, I could not fall asleep well. However, Ivan never again visited my room during that trip, and upon our arrival to Kharkiv, the incident seemed to evaporate as fast as it appeared. I never mentioned it to my parents, thinking it was not worth the commotion, but my mind continued to wonder about what I had done so wrong to upset my coach. To this day, I cannot answer that question, as no explanation had followed the event.

As awful as the above experience was, the worst began later. I just turned ten when Ivan's true colors were illustrated, although some players might have experienced his rage of similar magnitude earlier. During our first trip to Elektrenay, Lithuania, in the summer of 1988, our coach held a training camp. The trip lasted four to five weeks, which was plenty of time for him to weed out the weaker individuals. One morning, within the second week of the camp, we got up and the day began as usual. However, I noticed that a small group of players would not approach the rest of us and always maintained their distance. They would also be very quiet and not respond to any of our questions. This pattern continued for the remaining part of the day, until all were gathered by Ivan for the evening meeting in the same room. As we sat down, the exclusive group of players stood aside in one row, performing a Nazi-style salute by extending their arms forward. Seeing such a scene gave me shivers, and I understood that something serious was happening. Nobody would make a sound and the room reminded me of a cemetery during a funeral. Ivan walked into the room, passing through the middle with a smirk on his face. He sat down in his chair in the corner of the room, facing all of us, and exclaimed, "Heil Hitler!" The exclusive group of players responded in the same manner and repeated the phrase. Their faces turned red and their eyes were staring at the floor, trying to hide them from anyone's view. Ivan's face lit up and, at this point, he was smiling in their direction. Then, looking around at the rest of us, he asked, "Have you noticed something different?" No one would respond, as no one understood the reason for this question or why those players stood in the Nazi pose. Perhaps we were afraid to draw Ivan's searching eyes and become his next victims in whatever happened with the standing group in front of us. Ivan continued this meeting without elaborating on the situation, but occasionally saying "heil Hitler" and forcing the selected group to repeat the same. He would also occasionally remind them to fix their hair, combing it to the left in the same manner as Hitler. As the meeting went on, Ivan seemed more and more entertained. After each time the boys said "heil Hitler," he smiled and forced them to say it again several times in a row. The meeting was long. It lasted several hours in the manner described above.

When it ended, everyone spread into their rooms to sleep. However, not only could I not fall asleep after such an experience, but others moaned and groaned as well (we slept four per room). After about an hour or so, I heard the footsteps toward our door. As they approached, my heart sank. Ivan opened the door and turned on the light. He "woke up" one of my room-mates first and began testing his loyalty. I tried not to betray myself and lay in my bed very still with eyes shut. I heard everything that happened to my team-mate, so when my turn came, I was aware and prepared for what came next. As Ivan "woke" me up, he asked me if I loved him. I pretended not to under-stand what he meant after hearing my other roommates' responses, so I sat in my bed quietly. This ignited him a bit, so the next time he asked the same question, with a higher tone and more demeanor, I quickly responded "yes," being scared out of my wits of the next event. The next thing I heard was, "Prove it." Although I knew the response, I still asked him, "How?" Immediately, I was directed toward our window (we stayed on the fourth or fifth floor). I was then to climb the window ledge and, eventually, jump down off it. As I walked toward it, my legs felt like lead and my heart was pounding to the point it seemed ready to burst out of my chest. I approached it and froze for a moment. Ivan commanded me to open the window and climb out to the edge. I looked down and quickly began estimating my fall. I looked at a location with the most abundant grass, so my landing could be somewhat softer. I also looked at the trees that were fully covered by leaves and consid-ered them to be my other alternative for landing. They were some distance away from my position, and there was a possibility of me landing on the as-phalt sidewalk several feet before them. If I pushed my feet hard enough off the wall, I decided I could reach the softness of the trees, and therefore, land with fewer injuries. The second alternative became my choice. I slowly climbed the window's ledge and sat down on the edge, mentally preparing for the worst. I kept my eyes on the landing target and hoped to avoid the asphalt sidewalk. Sitting there for some time, my focus had drifted me away and I lost track of time. I had probably been sitting there for about a minute or a minute and a half when Ivan grabbed me from behind and pulled me by the shirt back inside. Several minutes went by before my mind could think clearly. Ivan set me on the bed and began asking me if I was really going to jump off the window. I responded "yes" and immediately was praised for my deed. I passed the test and felt very proud of myself. The next morning, I noticed that only a few players were talkative and realized that Ivan spent the whole night testing every one of us. In the evening, we gathered for another meeting. The group from the previous night had become much bigger, and now most of the players stood in the Nazi pose extending their hands forward and fixing their hair to the left. The meeting continued in a similar fashion as the night before. Ivan would randomly say "heil Hitler," and the standing players had to salute and repeat the statement.

Ivan was not satisfied by only few meetings of this nature. After the "testing," we gathered in one room for meetings each night. For the rest of the trip, our team would be divided into groups, and those who fell into the Nazi group continued to be ridiculed and humiliated by Ivan. Eventually, our coach's "amusement" was extended further. He began stratifying the ranks of the Nazi group and divided them into important and non-important members. After a few days, he emphasized one player to be the most important Nazi and declared him Fuhrer. The rest were his subordinates. As the trip went on, Ivan had another test for all who did not originally pass. I do not know what the test was, as no one spoke a word about it and I never gathered enough strength to ask. After its completion, several players redeemed themselves and were allowed to leave the Nazi group. Toward the end of the trip, our coach decided to elevate the humiliation and abuse and instructed one of the "Nazi" members to be the recipient of Temnaya, which will be discussed later. This was the first of four Temnayas I witnessed with my own eyes. All were instigated, supervised, and performed by our devoted coach. Other humiliating acts included "Nazi" members "shooting" everyone else in the room by pointing their fingers in all directions, imitating German soldiers during WWII against Soviet citizens. There were acts on a smaller scale directed at particular "Nazi" members to illuminate their "terrible" characteristics as human beings.

To my knowledge, none of the players mentioned these events to their parents. In our culture, being labeled a "Fascist" was one of the worst stigmas on your name. No one wanted to remember it happened. As I think of it now, I do not really know why I was willing to jump, but I was relieved and proud of myself afterward. Ivan thought he tested my loyalty, but instead he just tested my fear of being labeled a fascist. This test separated us and made one group (who passed) contemptuous toward the other (who did not pass). During our regular meetings, Ivan constantly came up with new ways to humiliate the Nazi group. Although I was not one of them, I am sickened thinking of how I could allow myself be brainwashed by the tyrannical maniac who used our young and naïve souls for his sadistic purposes. Perhaps Pravilov thought he was providing us with life lessons, but really, he was using torture to eliminate the weak players from the team. For some reason, I believed his words and gave no second thought about the wrongfulness of the whole situation. In my mind, the members of the Nazi group were traitors to our countrymen, exactly like Ivan said.

The Follow Up

After the Elektrenay trip, the entire dynamic of our team had changed, and Ivan had fully embraced his unorthodox methods of developing players and raising children. He truly believed we needed such treatment and thought that without strong punishment and constant reprimanding, nothing good would come of us. He told us our parents did not deserve to be called our parents, as they had done nothing but simply gave us birth and allowed us to exist. He really believed they were weak and unworthy. Furthermore, Pravilov proclaimed the goodness of his intentions and actions and declared himself our savior in the face of negligence and passivity.

All players on the team experienced some sort of "testing" on Ivan's behalf. Some stayed, but most left. As I think about it now, at any point of our team's existence, at least one or two players endured constant humiliation and abuse bombardment. He would alienate the rest of the team toward those players and make sure that no one would talk to them or associate with them in any way. Occasionally, parents would get involved. In response, he would brainwash our minds against the involved parents, and confront these parents through bullying. The incidents would not end with our parents alone; we would also be subjected to his ridicules and abuses as a reminder to not allow our parents to do so. If a parent revolted, the player paid the price. After a while, most parents would back away and ignore the situation. With time, Ivan truly became a master of bullying and continued this pattern throughout his coaching career for Druzhba-78.

Ivan's use of humiliation and physical abuse had increased significantly. He created degrading nicknames for the players. He would make up insulting jokes in front of the rest of the team about a player's certain abnormalities, physical or otherwise. Frequently, players would have swollen cheeks or colored eyes after a punishment had been doled out. With time, I was used to his ways and learned to block his insulting remarks, unless they were threatening and I believed I could seriously get hurt. One of those instances happened not long after the Elektrenay trip, during a practice. My technical performance in one of the drills illustrated no improvement and Ivan began to show signs of great impatience toward me. I could not control the puck the way he wanted me to, so he commanded me to take off my hockey gloves and extend my bare hands in front of him. As soon as I did so, he swung his hockey stick with full force and made contact on the back sides of my hands. I stood my ground, but the pain was unbearable and tears began to escape from my eyes. Noticing them, Ivan became furious and called me out to be a sissy. He instructed to continue holding my hands extended in front of him. There was a second swing, but this time, I intuitively dodged it by taking my hands away. This re-action did not go well with our coach and, in an instant, his mood turned into an uncontrollable rage. His emotions took over him and he began hitting my hands at will. The stick connected several times against the back part of my palms and the pain became too much to endure. I was scared but, at the same time, decided not to complain. *What would my father think of me?* I thought to myself at that moment. To teach me a further lesson, Ivan called in the rest of the team and instructed them to line up to shoot on net. Without protective hockey gloves, I was instructed to get in goal and save pucks with my bare hands. For each puck that I could not save, I would receive a blow with the stick on my bare hands. Since some of the players could shoot fairly hard by now, I could only imagine the severe pain I was facing. I made an attempt to save the first shot, which almost paralyzed my entire hand with the aftershock. On the second shot, my hand instinctively dodged the puck, and it went straight into the net. As soon as this happened, Ivan wasted no time in re-minding me of the consequences by laying a quick blow with his hockey stick. My entire arm went numb. I tried to save another puck, but it went through my hand like it was not even there. This resulted in another direct hit from Ivan, after which I noticed I could not hold my hand still. It shook violently like a nervous tick in front of my own eyes. Ivan was not satisfied and in-structed the players to shoot at my other side, so I could save the puck with my good hand. The scene repeated. This continued for a while until Ivan de-cided to send me to the locker room. There, I began changing my gear when Pravilov showed up and locked the door behind him. His exact words were, "Are you trying to escape from punishment?" Without hearing a response, he used his hockey stick to provide a few more blows to my bare hands. Then, he decided I needed to experience a "stick massage" and commanded me to stand sideways toward him. After several blows, there was a knock on the door from the players returning from the ice. While walking to open the door, he said in a hissing voice with staring, bulging eyes, "To be continued."

When every player was in and comfortably located in his seat, Ivan an-nounced that I betrayed my teammates and deserved to be punished. He told me to stand up in front of the team sideways toward him. He instantly swung his stick and connected it on my buttocks several times. To add to the insult and humiliation in front of my teammates, Ivan called me fascist and other names that would come to his mind. After the incident, my arms were in excruciating pain and I ended up with a cast on my left hand from a fracture. Considering the viciousness of Ivan's use of his hockey stick, I was actually surprised to find that my right hand had gotten away with only a big bruise, although the impact was felt for many days afterward. The incident did not go unnoticed by the players and, as a result, they stopped associating with me. For whatever reason, they showed no emotion or compassion for what happened that day. My isolation lasted several days before anyone on the team spoke a word toward me, but then everything seemed to return to normal. The misery ended as quickly as it started.

With time, the situations of Ivan's rage became more and more frequent and no player could escape his wrath. At random, he would pick on a certain player for a period of time and then take on another target. There was no way to predict when Ivan would decide I needed a treatment for my "bad" behavior.

My next major fallout with Pravilov happened about a week later that winter, as a result of the team's vote for captaincy. Our former captain lost his position after the Elektrenay trip, and after several months Ivan announced there would be a vote for a new one. Three players were nominated as finalists for the position, and I was one of them. On the day of the final results, Ivan revealed that I was not picked to be a captain. Soon after, we played a game against a team of players one year our senior and my personal performance, in Ivan's words, could not have been any worse. In Ivan's mind, my poor performance reflected my envious state of mind for the captaincy, and I needed a lesson to make that go away. Well, I mentally prepared myself for the onslaught, but I had no idea of the magnitude of Ivan's rage. After the game, I was told not to sleep well as the next day would bring me many "surprises." I could not complain to my parents and ask to stay home, because all I would hear was I probably deserved what was coming and I should accept it like a man. As soon as the next day's practice began, Ivan wasted no time pointing out any of my mishaps as major downfalls. At one point, he called me over and began using his hockey stick like a tomahawk behind my knees, telling me to bend them more for a lower stance. Sometimes, as I skated by, he would swing the stick from behind me and connect it on my back. In those days, shoulder pads provided minimal protection in the back and the blow described above made a significant impact, to say the least. The blow would have a resounding echo throughout the rink, and I could only imagine how the other players felt after witnessing such a scene. However, this onslaught was not anywhere close to what waited for me after the practice. When all players left for home, I was instructed to stay behind in the locker room and wait for Ivan's return.

After about fifteen long minutes, my coach finally came back and locked the door behind. He instructed me to do squats for as long as I could do them. After about a hundred or so, he left and told me not to stop. I continued to perform my squats, as I believed that he was somehow still watching me. When I reached about four hundred of them, he returned and locked the door. As I continued "exercising," Ivan grabbed a nearby hockey stick and sat at my side. Obviously, I already figured out what was coming next and prepared for the physical pain. During each squat down, Ivan swung his stick and connected on my buttocks, all the while telling me that this treatment was the only way to get rid of my envy toward the captains. The first ten blows were excruciating, but then each consecutive blow provided less pain, as my body had somehow become accustomed to it. After a long series of this "treatment," Pravilov stopped his physical abuse and began his familiar questionnaire about who I loved the most. Initially, I was silent, knowing this mind game was a losing situation for me regardless of my response. Through experience, I understood that, eventually, Ivan would always twist the story and manipulate my answers in a way where the punishment was inevitable. So, after the first question of who I loved the most, he became enraged of my stillness and called me retarded. He instantly used the stick in his hands to deliver a blow to my head. In a few seconds, I felt blood dripping on my face and thought this would stop his rage. But no, he repeated the question a second time. Seeing no other solution, I responded that I loved him the most, trying to satisfy his ego. The next question he asked was, "What about your parents? Don't you love them the most?" At this point, I found myself caught in my reply, because if I answered "yes," he would call me a liar, and if the answer was "no," he would still find a way to manipulate the situation to result in more punishment. Consequently, I resorted to "yes" with the idea that it was better to be punished sooner than later. As I expected, Ivan called me a liar and delivered a series of lighter blows on my head that resulted in another flow of blood.

At this point, I thought perhaps he would stop the onslaught, as I remember that my face was covered in red. Again, I was wrong. The next step for me was to wash my face in the sink. When I approached him later, as instructed, Ivan demanded that I prove my love for my parents. I was to strip naked and run out in the hallway yelling, "I love my parents; I love my parents." Trying to get out of this mess sooner, I did what I was told and went toward the door to complete my "assignment." Just as I was ready to open the door, Pravilov stopped me and became mad. In his words, I tried to get him in trouble in front of other people and send him to jail. For that, I was told to continue my squatting exercise standing naked and sideways toward him. The punishment continued with several blows on the buttocks with the flat part of the hockey stick blade. With the blood pouring down my face, with my buttocks not feeling a thing anymore (I had lost the count of the hits), I saw no way out of Ivan's grasp. Any response, anything I would do was just another way for Ivan to find my fault with me and resume his punishment. I also lost track of time and hoped that my parents would become concerned enough about my whereabouts to call the rink. This would save me from further embarrassment and humiliation, not to mention physical abuse. But the call never came, because there were many other nights when Ivan held us back for a long evening, and such an instance was a norm. My survival from this torture depended only on my own strength and will.

Eventually, after several hours of this torturous and tormenting lesson, the abuse stopped and Ivan told me to put my clothes on. All of a sudden, without any warning, he became the good guy and asked me, "Why would you let me do that to you?" I could not understand this sudden change in attitude toward me and stood there without a sound. I still believed this could be a trap and decided not to respond at all. In that instant, my coach approached me and gave me a long hug. I could not believe my own eyes and ears, but he looked and sounded genuine in his plea. Taking my arm in his hand, he walked me toward the sink and began washing dried blood off my face and wounds on my head. Then, he sat me down on one of the benches next to himself and told me not be envious ever again in a low and comforting voice. As it happened, I made no sound. I promised myself not be trapped again. After what seemed like a long pause, Ivan said that it was enough for that day. He took my navy blue *Dynamo* hat out of my jacket pocket and put it over my head, meanwhile comforting me that the worst was already behind and I should not be afraid of him anymore. To me, everything in the end sounded superficial. I still could not trust his words. *He just beat the crap out of me*, I thought to myself during his comforting lecture. I let him speak out and soon found myself on the other side of the locker room door, walking toward the exit of the rink.

On the way home, I pondered over the incident and could not understand Ivan's drastic change in attitude and behavior. I understood that complaining at home would not make any difference, so I decided to come up with a simple explanation. Upon my late arrival at home, I told my parents that a puck hit my head and I spent extra time with Ivan in the locker room trying to stop the bleeding. My mother said nothing in response and instructed me to undress. The blood on my head had soaked the hat, and she needed to use scissors to remove it. Because of the significant amount of blood, my mother became very concerned. She told me to get in the shower and she would address the wounds afterward. The cast on my hand from Ivan's recent beating prompted my mother to help me undress, and what both of us saw made us gasp in awe. My rear was completely black. Not to raise any suspicion about the incident, I kept quiet, hoping that the event would be simply forgotten. The blackness spread so wide that even the underwear could not hide the wounds. Not saying anything, with an inquiring and suspicious look on her face, my mom directed me to the shower and began preparing to care for the head wounds. Because of the green ointment (zelenka) my mother used on my head, I did not want other children to see it. For about five to seven days, I spent my school days in a hat, pretending I had caught a cold. My teammates knew I had wounds on my head, but I do not believe they wanted to know what happened that night behind closed doors. They probably feared learning the potential outcome, should they become Ivan's next unlucky victim. During my recent trip to Ukraine, my mother told me that she actually bought the story about the puck, which is why she did not question me further.

Less dramatic incidents of this sort continued to happen without any sign that Ivan might slow down. He would pick a player for a period of time and use him as a scapegoat. I was no exception and periodically would become the recipient of mental and physical abuse. The stories repeated themselves over and over, and describing each one would only be redundant. Ivan either used his hockey stick or his fists on our bodies like they were his punching and hitting bags. The treatment of players in such way became his trademark and every one of us soon accepted them as the norm. However, there is another fact worth mentioning about Ivan's unique ways of developing hockey players. Throughout my ten years with him, he tried to teach us toughness by resorting to what he called a "Canadian" type of hockey. Since our first days on the ice, we scrimmaged each other frequently with instructions to use any means to take the opponent down. This meant there were no rules and anything could happen. Inevitably, one player would swing his stick at another and pandemonium would ensue. On several occasions, these games resulted in broken bones and various other injuries.

The development of our "toughness" did not end there. Eventually, our coach came up with another exercise that, according to him, would really make us fearless. Two players were to stand on the opposite sides of the ice and skate toward each other at full speed, colliding in the middle. If a player slowed down, on his next turn he had to hold his hands behind his back, while his opponent was instructed to use a hockey stick to take him down. Originally, this was performed along the width of the ice's surface, but with time, we performed this drill along the entire length of it. I was not particularly big or tough, and on one occasion, I was partnered with the player whom I believed was the strongest player on our team. On my very first try, I instinctively slowed down before the collision and instantly was victimized by Ivan's rage. He told me to do it again with hands behind my back, whereas the other player had a hockey stick and could use it to take me down. On the first turn, I received a cross check blow upon my chest that forced me to stay down, recovering for some time. On the second turn, I received a swing blow from my right side that landed on my arm between the elbow and the shoulder. I was surprised it did not break the bone, but the impact definitely numbed the entire length of my arm. With one arm dysfunctional, I proceeded with the exercise two more times with the same player, who mercilessly landed his stick along other parts of my body.

Simultaneously, there was another player who slowed down before his first collision and became the recipient of similarly repeated blows. In the end, Ivan made the two of us compete against each other in order to preserve some dignity in front of the rest of the team. While everyone was seated in anticipation, the other player and I positioned ourselves on opposite sides of the ice rink. The two of us could also use hockey sticks to take the other down. To me, such competition meant life and death. I did not want to be ridiculed for my weakness and decided to exert my entire strength upon my opponent. On Ivan's signal, both of us sped up toward each other and collided in the middle with a thunderous sound. Apparently, my adversary did not want to lose either and we rebounded in opposite directions, flying a few feet back. I remember seeing stars in my eyes and wondering how much of this my body could take. But at the same time, I became angry at my opponent that he would not budge. Both of us were determined not to lose. We competed again and again for about six or seven additional times, with Ivan on the side as a judge, enjoying every moment of it. He could not declare the winner as we persevered and each collision would be just as noisy as any preceding one. In the end, he announced a tie without a word of ridicule or further humiliation.

The practice immediately resumed. Standing in line for one of the exercises, I noticed that blood was dripping on the ice from beneath my face mask. I touched the skin on my chin and felt a big cut. At first, I let it be, thinking it was not serious. But instead of subsiding, the blood poured more heavily. Instantly, I remembered how after one of the collisions my opponent rebounded back with his skates flying in the air next to my face. My face mask, at that moment, jolted back and exposed the chin, at which moment the skate must have cut it with its sharp edge. After notifying my coach, I was told with an intimidating glare not to be a baby and continue as nothing happened. By the end of the practice, the neck of my jersey looked like I had gotten into a vicious fight, with red covering the front. As soon as I changed my gear, I went straight into the first aid office, from which an ambulance took me for medical care. I was always afraid of needles, and lying in hospital #104, my body shivered with fright upon seeing the crooked needle that would penetrate my skin. The doctor calmed me down by questioning how I could not be afraid of vicious collisions on the ice but scared to death when confronted with needles. Anyway, my chin was eventually repaired with six stitches. I felt proud of myself at the moment and could not wait to show the scar to my parents. My father smiled in response and said the scar would make me a step closer to becoming a real man.

This "collision drill" had become a norm for our coach. He used it frequently against those who either showed some fright in battles for the puck or dissatisfied his other rules and instructions. However, he could only administer it back home in Kharkiv. When we travelled abroad, Ivan understood that such exercise would not sit well with whoever hosted our team. Consequently, he incorporated a new invention that extended the purpose of building that toughness. In the locker room, with and sometimes without protective equipment on, a player (who had earned punishment for some reason) was to run across the room into the wall with full speed. He performed a "body check" against it in order to feel no pain and fear when colliding with someone else on the ice.

The locker room version of this drill would occur either before, during, or after games, behind locked doors without arousing suspicions. Some players performed this madness more often than others, and most times for reasons other than being scared. Luckily, I did it only once. Certainly, a reasonably sane person would not come up with such methods, claiming their worth for developing super hockey players. Ivan constantly applied fear and intimidation, but always represented himself abroad as an ingenious coach who through his "high moral standards and unique training methods" performed wonders for those who wanted to reach their next level of performance.

Temnaya

As I mentioned earlier, the Elektrenay trip was a significant turning point for the players of Druzhba-78. Ivan would frequently pick a player for a certain period of time and terrorize him through both his mind and body. When the player had undergone a series of abuses and humiliations, Pravilov would eventually take a softer approach to smooth the transition from being an "unworthy" member of the team to becoming a fully deserving one. Such a transition could be sudden or very gradual, but no player was immune to those "tests." To make things worse, Ivan continued to elevate the level of his abuses to new heights. One of them happened several times over the course of the existence of Druzhba-78, and only a few players became the recipients. However, all the players on the team at that moment witnessed and experienced it. For confidentiality purposes, I will not reveal specific details regarding the location, timing, or the names of the players directly involved. The story, however, must be told for others to learn valuable lessons and understand the true nature of Druzhba's coach. The memories in my mind are so vivid that I see them as if they occurred yesterday.

Sometimes, after a player had been picked on for a long period of time, Ivan would decide he needed a greater form of punishment. This always happened when we were away on a trip, when the players had no access to their parents. At one of the team meetings (Ivan ran them almost every night, with all players gathered in the same room, behind locked doors), our coach announced that the player needed a complete purification from his "bad" deeds. He began by explaining the gang rules that governed the streets. Under these "rules," a person at fault was to receive a brutal beating from the rest of the gang. What happened next to that person would be at the discretion of the members. As always, Ivan would remind us of all the alleged negative traits and bad deeds of the player in focus. He would mock him and humiliate him in front of the team and then let the players decide the verdict. Ivan's word was the last one, and those that hesitated in their decision would be instigated or persuaded by questions like "Don't you believe he deserves the worst punishment for his betrayal toward you?" or "How could you let him be unpunished when he desires the same treatment for you?" After Ivan announced the verdict for the player to be punished, we were to put a dark bag or sack over the player's head. That prevented him from seeing what was happening. Ivan would not be satisfied there. As humiliated and abused the player was, Ivan would remark, "See, the karma has fallen upon you and neither I nor anyone else can stop it. Look how angry your teammates are for your betrayal." The most disturbing thing about this was that Ivan was able to brainwash many and provoke them, including myself, to become contemptuous toward the player in focus. Only a few players actually had a complaint against the "punished" player, but that was personal. Ivan was able to channel their anger and use it against the one being punished. As a result, very few became the actual "butchers," but all witnessed the horrific scene.

As I explained earlier, it all began by putting a dark sack over the player's head. Those who could not wait let their fists fly from different directions at the face and the rest of the body. I remember being petrified by the scene and could not move a limb. I stood on the side and could not believe my eyes. The few who threw punches looked so infuriated that it seemed nothing could stop them. After about twenty-five to thirty seconds of receiving numerous blows in the face and the head, the player would fall on the floor. The punching crowd would begin using their legs and kicked wherever their feet could land. The "punished" player would cry, scream, and beg for mercy, but to no avail. In one instance, the player stood his ground and made no sound. The blows would continue, but he would not budge. Because of his silence, the beating lasted for a long time. Watching the scene on the side, I felt sorry for the punished teammate but did not do anything about it. Seeing the horrific picture in front of my eyes, I was afraid the same fate would follow me later. Defending him would be like suicide. In the meantime, Ivan would sit somewhere in the corner of the room and supervise the event, except for one time when he left the room and let the players take care of the rest. He would encourage the ones who stood still and tell them to get involved. Not everyone was up to the task, and most spent the time staring at the scene and not making any noise of their own. At one of the events, Ivan sat next to me and called me to approach him. He sat me on his lap while a small group of players brutalized the player in front of our eyes. With a smirk on his face, he asked me why I would not participate in the beating. I could not respond, thinking the question was rhetorical. But to be silent was not an option with our coach. "Isn't that what you want?" he persisted, and then added, "He has betrayed you and punished you with his lies, and you let him get away with it? There is no remorse for fascists, and you should demonstrate the magnitude of your hatred toward him." At that moment, I was probably terrified to respond in any manner and only stared at the scene in front of me. Surprisingly, Ivan let me off his lap and told me to get involved. I walked a couple of steps closer, but one way or another, I could not force myself to join in the madness. The beating would last for what seemed like an eternity and only stopped when Ivan decided it was enough.

For many days, the punished player's face would look like a boxer's who had just gone twelve rounds with an opponent, but I can only imagine how the rest of the body looked. When random people asked what happened to "that" boy, Ivan would always respond with a smile on his face and say, "He got into a fight with one of his teammates and got the worst of it." His responses were disturbingly casual. As far as I know, not one player has ever discussed the events described above, even among each other. I was not a recipient of this cruel reprimand, but it has continued to haunt my memories, as I know that at any time I could have been a victim. I could only imagine how the actual recipients felt and feel about it today.

The most disturbing thought about the entire scenario is that Ivan convinced the actual recipients of "Temnaya" that they were at fault. He made them feel worthless and degraded. He would tell them to apologize to the rest of the team for their betrayal. What betrayal? Only Pravilov knew. When the team would return home from the trip, the punished player personally visited each of his teammates' homes to ask for forgiveness. When I opened my door, as I recall, I did not know what to say. I knew the player was in a dire situation, but I also understood the consequences of my decision. Telling him he was forgiven would mean inviting the problem upon me and explaining my reasoning in front of the rest of the team. As a result, I chickened out and said what I thought everyone else on the team would say: no. The player looked me straight in the eyes and paused there for a moment, asking to forgive him without another word. I stood quiet, feeling sorry for him and myself. The player slowly turned around and silently walked away. I remember the excitement on my father's face that a teammate showed up at our door. He asked me to invite him in, but my facial expression probably told him not to intervene. I remember feeling scared and hateful toward myself, knowing that the tables could someday turn around and I would be the one asking the same teammate for forgiveness.

To say how manipulative Ivan was and how well he was able to brainwash our young and naïve minds (Temnaya began when we were nine and ten years old) would be an understatement. I believe he was building a machine similar to the Stalinist-era Communism, which was based on constant supervision, interrogation, and punishment of its subjects. Stalin used it to preserve his power and Ivan used it to hold his grip over each one of us. The more I learned about Soviet history, the more I became convinced that the regime within Druzhba-78 was too similar to be a mere coincidence. The expressions like "for the teammates" and "betrayal of players," for example, reflected slogans such as "in the name of the people" and "for the communist party" that were so abundant under Stalin's rule. "Temnaya" was just another horrible example that reflected the Soviet regime, and Ivan happily obliged his role as its executioner. He was able to alienate the rest of the team toward a certain player, and each year he became more and more masterful at this enterprise. For all my years on Druzhba-78, he was able to affect each of my responses, and to say they were mine would be hypocritical. Thus, I always responded "no" when expected to do so—and responded "yes" when I saw and felt his approval. Recalling the whole scenario of the player's plea for forgiveness, I would love to go back and change my response. Only when Pravilov gave us a green light to have normal relations with the player in focus would we change our attitude instantly. When this instant arrived, it seemed like the whole experience just evaporated and we became friends again.

Alushta

While I was a member of Druzhba-78, time moved very slowly. I never felt comfortable with my performance on and off the ice and could never trust Ivan about what awaited me next. Each day was another day to live through, and I simply tried to come out of it unscathed. Soon, the incidents similar to the captains' vote continued to pile up, only with less viciousness and time to endure. Ivan never ceased to surprise us with new ways to damage his players' morale and self-esteem. By the time I turned eleven in the summer of 1989, the team prepared to travel for the long four-week training camp in Alushta. Because the town was on the shores of the Black Sea in the Crimean Peninsula, the trip, according to my parents and Ivan himself, was supposed to be fun. But fun was never part of Ivan's plan.

Ivan arranged for all of us to sleep in the wrestling gym. Each player brought his own cot and Ivan decided who would sleep in which corner. The first couple of weeks went without an incident, and I believe, after the mid-point of our trip, our coach decided to spice it up a little. One evening, before one of our routine runs (three-fourths of a mile with hills), Ivan said that the last three players would continue to run. Being a slow runner, I came in third from last and prepared to run again. Ivan would not let us go right away, but asked us to make a choice. The first option would be to continue running and the second to sleep standing in the gym in front of everyone. The thought of such humiliation in front of the team would be unbearable; therefore, I decided to run again. One of us, however, chose otherwise and stood aside watching. After the third player and I completed our second run, Ivan suddenly told the three of us to leave for our quarters. I was very glad for choosing the first option because, I thought then, I would not have been strong enough to face what was coming. In addition, the sisters of two other players were also with us and were watching the shame as well. Upon our return, everyone else was already preparing for bed and we joined them. When Ivan came back, the "fun" began. He instructed the player who chose the option of not running to get in the middle of the gym, climb the thick gym rope, and stay there. It had a knot on the bottom, so he could actually comfortably hang on by crossing his legs. As the player climbed, he was told to tell all of us a good night story. Because he could not come up with anything, Ivan asked him if he read any books lately. He replied, "Yes, and I have it with me." Ivan became amused and laughingly commanded whoever slept next to that player to search for the book and bring it to him. I am not sure how the player on the rope felt at the moment, but I tried to fall asleep feeling glad that was not me. The name of the book was *Carlson*. The main character of the story had a propeller in his back and was one of the favorites for children of my generation. Soon my teammate on the rope began telling the story, and about midway through, Pravilov asked him if he was thirsty. After hearing the positive response, our coach instructed another player to carry a bottle of Pepsi-Cola to the storyteller. After few sips, he was to hold the bottle in his hands anyway possible by hanging onto the rope and continue the story. I fell asleep shortly after relishing the moment of peace and quiet in my mind. I never found out how long the storyteller spent on the rope. The next morning, he woke up in his bed. I blocked the thought out of my mind, knowing he likely compromised some of his privileges on the team in order to sleep in bed.

The next morning, we proceeded with training like nothing happened. A few more days had gone by before Ivan decided to make the trip more interesting, at least for me. Similar to other instances, he would observe every one of my moves and look for any little thing to pick on. He would not ridicule me in isolation, believing everyone needed to see and hear how terrible and unworthy I was. He would make up some stories that several players gladly used against me in our personal conversations. He would point out my short fingers, for instance, and call them greedy. He would tell stories about how I could steal from others and my "greedy" fingers would always be enough to prove my guilt. He reminded everyone of the incident with one *kopeika*, which would be equivalent to one cent. During my first year on Druzhba-78, I was walking home from school with a couple of my teammates. Because I loaned one of them some money for a cupcake, I asked for the change of one *kopeika*. At that very moment, Ivan was walking toward us and I did not notice him. He overheard the conversation and began belittling me for worrying about one kopeika. Growing up in a family where each penny (*kopeika*) was accounted for, now I was confused about two opposing ideas: greed and appreciation for what I had. Ivan, of course, would not let it go and always reminded me how "greedy" I was.

Anyway, Ivan continued the barrage of verbal insults until, one day, they were no longer enough. After a day of "terrible" performance on the soccer field, he told me to stand aside from the other players. I could not hold a conversation with them, as I did not deserve their company. Similar to the incident with the rope, he instructed me to sleep that night standing next to my bed. I stood motionless for at least an hour, when Ivan pointed his flashlight at me. That sobered me up quickly and I straightened my body from a crooked stance. He made a hissing sound, calling me to approach. I did so and saw an angry face. "What are you doing? Are you bad?" he furiously asked. I could not understand his question, but answered, "I did what you told me to." Pravilov got up, leaning toward me, and said, "Are you saying I made you sleep standing up?" Without waiting for my response, he grabbed my neck with one of his hands and began squeezing his fingers. Choking, I made an attempt to lean back and get out of it, but his grip would not give way. Now, Ivan stood up above me, saying, "I should kill you right now for blaming me for what you did to your teammates." I thought to myself that Ivan honestly had gone mad and was about to kill me. I felt my face turning red, and perhaps other colors, but that would not stop his onslaught. I had no idea what I had done to my teammates, and if Ivan considered my poor performance on the field as deserving of death, he surely must be insane, I thought. At that moment, I was just waiting for him to end me. Having so many witnesses around calmed me down, although I am not sure if anyone overheard us. For some reason, I was not fighting him. I accepted my fate and imagined him going to prison. *What a scene would that be?* I wondered. I could not argue with a madman, especially with one who had his hand wrapped around my neck trying to kill me. My coach began calling me all kinds of names including fascist, traitor, ungrateful, Jew, etc. While holding my neck in his hand, he began dragging me toward the restroom across the gym. My feet barely held their ground and I struggled to gain some balance underneath. His other free hand held a flashlight that guided the way, and as soon as we got in, he dropped me on the floor.

Laying there helpless I began recovering, but not for long. The next second, Ivan made a swing with his leg and stopped right before kicking my stomach. I guess he did not want others to hear the beating, considering two players' sisters were present, and changed his mind. His frozen stance held for few seconds, with his foot a couple of inches from my stomach. The look on his face was intimidating. His eyes stuck out and the saliva flew out of his mouth in rage. I had already learned that this was his go-to move, so in return, I pretended to be scared. The next moment, Ivan declared I needed to redeem myself and prove my loyalty to my teammates. He leaned down toward me and said, "Eat shit." I hesitated for a moment, and for that received, a blow on the back of my neck. Then he grabbed my neck again and dragged me toward the toilet. It contained some residual feces; Ivan demanded that I eat it. Next, he asked me if I loved my teammates, to which I responded "yes." "So eat shit if you do," he barked at me, continuing to bulge his eyes out and repeating the hissing sound. I looked into the toilet for some time, mentally preparing for this humiliation. My coach, on the other hand, could not wait and grabbed my head from behind, pushing it into the toilet. He held me in this position for a while, until I received another even harder blow from behind, on my head. I slowly began to do what was instructed. Ivan continued "encouraging" me to clean the entire toilet with my tongue, wrapping his fingers around my neck and not letting me to back away. After some time, the toilet was clean. The next instant my coach grabbed my hair, pulling it back. "*Ny chto syka, nravitsa der'mo lizat'*" (So, Bitch, do you like to lick shit)?" he asked with an empowering smirk on his face. I did not respond. I stood on my knees, staring at the floor, keeping my eyes away from his view. For a moment, his mind seemed to ponder what punishment would be next. My body began to shiver. Based on Ivan's furious facial expression, he was ready to annihilate my weak existence. His next assignment soon followed.

I was told to kiss his feet to prove that I loved him. I pushed myself forward, sliding my knees along the hard-tiled floor. Like a slave gazing down and not daring to look up, I performed this act and was ready to burst out with emotions. By now, my self-esteem could not drop any lower. Ivan had achieved what he intended. He subdued me to his will. The next question was about my parents, and of course, I replied that I loved them. "Who do you love more, them or me?" he quickly asked me. I suspected the question was a trick and saw no other option but to be quiet. The idea was not successful. Ivan showed no patience and grabbed me by the neck again. Both of his hands had their fingers wrapped around my throat in a deadly grip. That very second, I changed my mind and decided to respond, but I was one second too late. No word could come out of my mouth, because the grip was tight enough to cut off all sound. Instinctively, I grabbed both of his hands with my arms, trying to loosen the grip, but to no avail. With intense hatred in his eyes, Ivan began covering me with words like "fascist" and "traitor." After about thirty to forty seconds of this physical and verbal onslaught, Pravilov let his fingers loose and told me never to be quiet again when asked a direct question. In fear and confusion, I said that I loved him more. "So now you do not love your parents, huh?" he quickly followed my response. I told him I loved them, but not as much as him. At this point, I saw no logic in Ivan's reasoning and began to accept my fate of being blamed in any case, regardless if it would make sense or not. The next moment, Ivan lost his control. He threw a few punches onto my face and called me a liar, although I could not understand why. I stuck to my responses for a while until I decided to change the tactic and tell my coach that I loved my parents more. As soon as I did so, I realized my huge mistake. That infuriated him further, because now he saw me trying to outsmart him. He called me a liar again for reversing the story and laid a series of punches into my stomach. As he spoke, Ivan's face turned red and saliva flew into my face from his mouth. His tone was sharp and his words were cruel, to say the least. He called me a chameleon and a Jew, constantly repeating that I changed my colors like a chameleon and attempted to wiggle myself out of the punishment like a Jew would. Standing on my knees in front of my coach, I promised myself to be quiet for the rest of the night. I knew I would receive a few more blows, which I did, but better to get this over with sooner than later.

Shortly after, for no apparent reason, the atmosphere had suddenly changed. Again, I could not understand the logic, but I was happy the beating had ended. Ivan helped me up to my feet and gave me a prolonged hug. I could not believe what was happening and thought it was another trick. But he continued to hold me and asked me if I really loved him and my teammates (he did not mention my parents). I said "yes" and began weeping. A similar situation happened during my punishment after the captains' vote, and this had become a routine. I continued to be distrustful. He could return to his old self at any second without warning. My experience with Ivan taught me not to take anything for granted, and expecting the worst would always give me a better chance of survival. I listened to his preaching until he let me go to bed and was glad the charade was over.

I could not speak much to any of my teammates for the rest of the trip. The girls would ask me why my mood was always grim and why I would not smile. All I could say was for them not to bother me and go on with their interests. The humiliation I experienced made me rethink about continuing with Druzhba-78, and I decided that upon our return home, I would quit immediately. When we returned home, I told my parents of my decision. But instead of hearing their support, I heard, "If you decided so, you must tell this to your coach in person." I was mortified. I was not ready to confront him, and my parents were not helpful. As a result, I made no such move.

The rest of the years I spent with Ivan, only one more incident (in Uzhgorod) could top this humiliation for me. I had received vicious and brutal beatings that turned my cheeks purple and swollen, I was ridiculed in public for all my deficiencies, I listened to embarrassing and ridiculing jokes from some of my teammates who repeated everything Ivan said, but the thought of being someone's slave and having to bow to their will would never leave my mind. Now, I have to live with this for the rest of my life.

Uzhgorod and the Aftermath

As each year went by, Ivan became a mastermind of manipulation and torture. Because our team usually shared ice with other teams, coaches and players on the opposite side witnessed many instances of his abuse. They saw him use his hockey stick on our bodies as if chopping wood in preparation for a cold winter. They saw him make a mockery out of us for all to see and hear. Many officials and coaches saw and knew his behavior on the ice and his punishments toward the players, but everyone chose to look the other way rather than intervene. Players from other teams would confront us saying we looked and acted like programmed robots, and Ivan held the remote controller manipulating each of our movements. They would ask us, "Why are you so afraid of your coach?" They would tell us that we never spoke without Ivan's permission, that we defended him despite the fact that he beat and humiliated us in front of them. That was until a couple of them eventually ended up on our team and experienced his wrath firsthand. In the meantime, Ivan became more confident in his invincibility and was more prone to show his rage in public. Again, because no one wanted to deal with him, he would just simply walk away and continue his torment.

By now I was almost twelve. In May, at the end of the 1989–90 school year, our team prepared to leave for a training camp. We traveled to Uzhgorod, a small city near the western border of Ukraine, and stayed there about six weeks. Soon after we loaded the train in Kharkiv, my problems began to pile up. The trip to Uzhgorod took an entire night and everybody settled for a good night's sleep, except for me. Ivan approached my bunk and sat me upright, telling me to wake up. He slapped me on the face a couple of times and said, "You were going to bed without saying good night, weren't you?" I could not believe my ears, because just moments ago he explicitly commanded everyone to hit the sack. While this thought went through my mind, he slapped me few more times, repeating, "Are you awake, are you awake?" To add to my amazement, he stuck his eyes out and began the familiar hissing and intimidating sound. I could not understand what I did wrong and why he jumped on me for no apparent reason. At the moment I thought, *I guess it is my turn to be ridiculed and abused. I only hope it will not be as cruel as some other players experienced before me.* Our one-way conversation resumed with similar questions like "Who do you love the most?" and "Why don't you love your parents the most?" These are the same questions that terrorized me a couple of years earlier. Because I was reluctant to respond, Ivan landed several fists on my face to get something out of me. I kept quiet, knowing that the beating would be there regardless of my reactions to his questions, and the quicker he got it over with, the sooner I would get to sleep. The bruises on my face that would shine the next day affected me very little. Ivan had a talent of convincing others of some irrelevant story that happened to us. So, I took the beating and accepted my fate of being a target for the rest of that trip. I had no idea how vicious my coach planned to be.

The first three weeks went by with minor incidents, because Ivan had two other players as his priority targets. For some time, they were not allowed to go to the bathroom. They were to urinate into a two-liter pop bottle and then drink it. They performed, upon Ivan's command, some very humiliating and degrading acts in front of the team. They crawled on all fours like dogs, barking and kissing Ivan's and other players' feet. They would fight each other on the trampoline below us for the title of being the second worst human being on the planet. The fights would last for a long time, and the boys would seriously beat each other. They would fight for the right to go to the bathroom. They would also fight for the right to drink water, instead of their own urine. Not a day went by without bruises and swollen faces for both of them.

One day, during one of the humiliating sessions in front of everyone's eyes, Ivan instructed both players to show their urine-soaked underwear. The scene was disgusting. We found out that Ivan forbade both players to wash their clothes and instructed them to wear the same underwear day after day. Considering that they were not allowed to use the restroom more often than not, their undergarments smelled horrible. So in front of all the players, they were to hold up their filthy underwear, allowing each of us to smell the stench. Then for no apparent reason, Ivan began instructing one of the two boys to walk toward me and stick the underwear in my face. I was appalled, and not by the disgusting smell, but by Ivan's twisted mind and his definition of entertainment. He smiled widely, telling the player to stand in that position for some time. Some players took great enjoyment in what they saw. They laughed and smiled. I sat there motionless, hopefully giving Ivan no further twisted amusement. I thought of the two players in focus who endured tremendous humiliation and could only imagine their fates when Ivan confronted them. The player stood in front of me, holding his underwear for about two minutes, when Ivan asked him to lay it on my head. Those who were laughing found this even funnier. At that moment, I realized that now, my turn for humiliation had arrived. Ivan's grin had not left his face since the beginning of this charade. I tried to look the other way and turned my head in different directions. But instead of relieving myself of everyone's gaze, I provoked harder laughs and further humiliation. After a few moments, the player standing in front of me was ordered to leave me alone and pick up his underwear. For a moment I felt relieved, hoping this was one of the random entertainment sessions we were so used to by now. Shortly after, though, my suspicions about Ivan's personal rage toward me had been realized.

Gradually, I became the focus of his jokes and constant ridicules. When my turn arrived, the entire world seemed to have fallen upon me in an instant. During our fourth week in Uzhgorod, Ivan became exceptionally attentive to all my moves and what I spoke, although I kept it to a minimum. As usual, he began his process of name-calling, public humiliation, and physical abuse on and off the ice. By the end of the fourth week, he decided to force me to put on a dress and told the rest of the team that my name had changed to a girl's name. Considering my baby faced look during my childhood years, I understood that some people could actually take me for a girl if given this perspective. Ivan saw that and used it against me. That decision came so suddenly that I could not comprehend if Ivan was serious, as he was smiling widely. Never, I remember thinking, had anyone on the team experienced this type of humiliation, and perhaps this could be a temporary "entertainment" within the enclosed doors. Some of the players on the team who disliked me for one reason or another picked up on it and began their charade. Ivan made me their puppet and forced me to obey all of their commands for the rest of the camp. They ordered me to wear the dress all day. Soon after, the team departed for lunch and, of course, I could not take the dress off. On the way there, I was kicked and punched by my "masters" and ridiculed by all means. Throughout the entire walk, I was hoping that a passerby would stop and intervene, but this never happened. After some time, I gave up on the thought and just prepared for the worst, thinking of all the terrible things that awaited me within the next two weeks. Nevertheless, the way my "masters" treated me bothered me the least. What struck me was Ivan's facial expression upon our arrival at the diner. Standing first in line, because Pravilov instructed "girls go first," our coach told the clerk that I was to receive the best meal. Thinking that I was a girl (Ivan referred to me in the girl's name), the clerk called me by that name and commented on the dress. When I looked up, I saw my coach with a very wide grin agreeing with the clerk. At that moment, I switched from the survival mode to anger and rage. I wanted to kill him right there on the spot. Ivan's grin turned into a loud laugh. I took my tray to a table and sat there without touching my lunch. All kinds of things had flown through my mind.

The laugh penetrated my skin like no other humiliation from my "masters." The worst thing was that I could do nothing about it. In my mind, my days on this team were over, but I needed to survive the final two weeks.

I could not imagine any worse humiliation. For the most part, it was a physical abuse. I was kicked and punched repeatedly. I was told to walk on the street in the dress Ivan ordered me to wear. My situation became helpless and hopeless, as the rest of the team had distanced themselves from me. Those who were my "masters" showed no remorse and, with each consecutive day, designed new ways to humiliate me in public. I had literally become their slave for the rest of the trip. At that moment, I began thinking of suicide. I saw no end to this torture and could not even sleep. My eyes became dark, but I could not tell if it was from the beatings or from the lack of sleep. I knew my father would not understand the true depth of the situation and would say I probably had it coming. My mother would have no strength to battle both my coach and my father. Therefore, I asked my "masters" to beat and kick me every time they wanted to humiliate me, so they could kill me sooner. To this they reacted with a loud laugh, telling me that such an end would be too easy. They wanted me to suffer and resorted to various tricks.

The abuse continued the rest of the trip. When my masters focused on something else, Ivan picked up their slack. When Pravilov used his attention on someone else, the masters resumed their entertainment with their slave. Eventually, when the last week approached, Ivan promised me a grand finale and that karma awaited me for my "betrayal." He also instructed my masters to back off and let him have the rest of the fun. The question of betrayal always lurked in my mind, as I could not understand exactly who I had betrayed. Ivan would never make it clear, and asking him would only add to my misery. Therefore, my final resort was to survive the onslaught and quit altogether upon my arrival home.

During the last week of our trip, the players were able to visit families of the local hockey team and sleep over at their homes until the last day. The two boys who had been abused at the beginning of the trip and I were left behind at the gym, where we slept on the second floor balcony. Each night, Ivan would come up with different ways to keep us from falling asleep. He would force us to fight on the trampoline on the first floor. He would make us tell the worst things about each other, all of which were false. When Ivan would leave for a while, the three of us coordinated our stories to make them believable for Ivan's sake. Then we would act them out in front of him to satisfy his thirst for "entertainment." It continued that way until three days before our departure home. That was my judgment night.

As all three of us pretended to be asleep under our blankets, not a sound could be heard. Then the footsteps approached my bed and the blanket flew off. Pretending to be asleep, I continued laying there motionless. I could hear Ivan's heavy breathing and knew from the sound of it that this would be a long night. He grabbed my shirt at my chest and lifted me up so I would sit upright facing him directly. Holding my shirt with one hand, he delivered a devastating punch with the other. It connected on my right jaw and made a clicking sound. The punch sobered me up quickly, although I expected it all along. I was mentally prepared for the worst and understood Pravilov would resort to far more vicious punishment than mere punches on the face. Immediately, Ivan threw a few more punches with words like *gnida* (lice), *tvar* (wretch), *predatel* (traitor), *fashist* (fascist), *evrey* (Jew), etc. At the moment, he was greatly infuriated and I thought steam would actually begin coming out of his ears. His face color changed from bright red to purple. While cursing, the saliva would fly in different directions. I truly believed that he could kill me and then get away with murder through some slimy excuse. With that in mind I decided to persevere and outlast the barrage of physical abuse. After several punches in the face, Ivan stopped for a moment to tell me that I could not get away with my betrayal and the punishment ritual must be performed in full. He said that the other two boys experienced a similar outcome and this night was my turn. He paused for about ten seconds and asked me what type of punishment I would like for myself. I told him I would not like any of it and, in response, received another two blows on the face. "You will not get away with anything. Haven't you realized already that karma is inevitable and I am here to fulfill that obligation as an executioner?" After almost four years of witnessing and experiencing Ivan's wrath, I was used to his ways of intimidation and abuse. But this time, I felt, was different and he could really kill me. Ivan became more persistent with the question about the type of punishment I preferred for myself. I stood still and would not utter a sound just like so many other times before, during Pravilov's private "sessions." He started pacing back and forth, contemplating his next move.

About thirty seconds went by before he stopped and instructed me to stand up facing him. My position was next to the railing on the second floor balcony that overlooked the gym on the first floor. I stood there motionless and thought that Ivan intended to throw me over the railing to teach me how to fly. But he had something else in mind. He decided to use me as a soccer ball during penalty kicks. For those who are not familiar with the soccer penalty kick, it is assigned to be performed by a player against the opposite goalie one on one. The ball is kicked toward the goal uninterrupted. In this situation, I was to be the ball. I tried to block that thought out of my mind, but the vision of him connecting his rubber-soled shoe with my stomach made me sick. On the very first try, he stepped a few paces back to gain momentum and instructed me to stand still. Then he set in motion and swung his leg with full force. My body reacted instantly and dodged the kick by leaning sideways. Pravilov's momentum carried him farther and his leg went over the rail, almost throwing him over it. He stumbled and I saw the scared look on his face. Without losing any time, he probably grabbed my head and knocked it against the railing, because at that moment, I lost consciousness for a few seconds. How wonderful the moment of my unconscious state was! As I recall, I dreamed of playing with my friends at my grandmother's place and was a happy child. But it did not last long, and my vision started to clear up.

Ivan's face was inches away from mine, and I believe he cursed me with all kinds of names and profanities. He told me I tried to kill him and that I deserved the same. The "session" resumed and Ivan positioned me away from the railing. This time I was instructed to keep my hands behind my back and not move an inch. He took about three or four paces back and, with full swing, landed his foot on my stomach. Instantly, I was out of breath and leaned over to regain it. Ivan could not wait for my recovery, and while I was bent forward and catching my breath, he connected another blow from underneath with his foot. This time he knocked me off my feet and I flew a few feet away on the floor. At that moment, he asked me if I was sick of him and if I wanted to quit the team. I responded, "Yes." The question and the response seemed to make no difference and the "penalty kicks" continued. After seven or eight blows, I stopped counting. But there were many and by the end, he performed between twenty and thirty of them. He made sure that each kick came with anticipation and paused before almost every one of them. To make them even more hurtful, he would take more paces back. The noise from the kicks would always make a resounding thump throughout the gym, and it could probably be heard outside the building. I noticed that birds would fly away from the window after each kick. At least half of the kicks forced me to lose my footing and fall on the floor. A few of them, just like after the first blow, were suddenly followed by repeated beating while I was in recovery. It seemed Ivan was eager to finish me off and could not wait for me to die. The end came as abruptly as the whole thing started. He stopped for few seconds and said it was enough for the night. He called me several different degrading names and said that fascists and traitors must be exterminated. On the final note, he added "to be continued" and walked away. I was stunned and perplexed at what just happened. I was angry beyond my mind, but I was also scared to do anything. In the end, I was simply relieved it ended. I did not know if anything in my body was broken, and I did not care. I just went to bed mentally preparing myself for the remaining two days and nights.

The next day, the three of us had plenty of time to ourselves, and the two other boys asked me to describe what Ivan did. I showed them my midsection, and for the first time since the previous night, I saw how badly I was damaged. My entire abdominal region had turned dark black. I could not twist my body in any direction, as the pain would be unbearable. I could not laugh, even if there had been something to laugh about. The boys also described their experiences with Ivan and made it clear that neither of them could escape his fury either. Actually, their stories topped mine on the scale of brutality and viciousness. They said they wet their beds because of the fear of walking in the hallway to the restroom. Their fear of him was greater than mine. One of the boys had lost his parents (they had passed away) and Ivan moved him into his own apartment. That thought alone frightened him more than anything because upon our arrival in Kharkiv, he would be living with the monster. They also told me they had several judgment nights in comparison with only one on my part, and that I probably had more coming my way. The news was not comforting, but I was determined to outlast Ivan's wrath. We discussed our next moves upon our arrival home. I told them I would quit right away. If my parents objected, I would run away from them. The thought of being anywhere near Ivan was unacceptable. Surprisingly, the two remaining days and nights flew by very quickly. We saw Ivan only occasionally and were left at the gym by ourselves. I used that time to think about what I would tell my parents and how I would escape Ivan's grasp. In the end, my parents held my future in their hands and I needed to convince them of my immediate departure from Druzhba-78.

Upon my arrival home, I told my parents I wanted to quit hockey and leave my team. I did not elaborate on my reasoning, but simply said I never wanted to be near Ivan again. Both of my parents, of course, were shocked at my decision, and began convincing me to return. "Your decision is absurd," they would repeatedly tell me and I should not quit what I started. My father called me a wimp and eventually repeated Ivan's exact words, that I was a fascist and a traitor. I realized that my parents had been in contact with Ivan all that time and were told stories that depicted my character in a negative light. Now, they were on his side, but what came next even I did not see coming.

They invited Ivan into our home, so he could personally convince me to come back. I never imagined such a thing could happen, as I never thought my parents would betray me. But I was wrong. I was preparing to go outside to play with my friends when the doorbell rang. The voices were quiet in the hallway, so I took no notice of someone's arrival. Then I heard a laugh that I could not mistake for anyone else's. Sure enough, Ivan entered the room and closed the door behind him. I could not believe my own parents left me in our own home with Ivan one on one. The situation forced me to think quickly and I vowed not to succumb to any promises. Again, I made a mistake. Ivan did not come to promise me immunity from my "masters." He did not apologize for his atrocities. He frankly said, "Are you mad? Do you think I could so easily let you get away? You made me come all the way here, and now you must pay." He began punching me in the face. I, in return, would not make a sound. Doing so would mean defeat. At that moment, I was no longer concerned with Ivan but with my own parents. I felt helpless and hopeless. Now, I could only rely on my own wits. I "confessed" to Ivan that I planned to get him in trouble. I told him my attempt at leaving was temporary. I saw no other way to get rid of him but to "confess" my fault in everything, although it was not true. That was the last straw for me, and even when Ivan was present in our house, I began planning my escape. My parents betrayed me and I could not rely on anyone else, as I believed they would conspire against me again in a similar fashion. When Pravilov "convinced" me to return, we came out of the room into the hallway where my parents awaited us. Ivan had a huge smile on his face and told them we solved our differences. "Now," he said, "everything will be fine and no one is leaving the team." He also gave me a prolonged hug while caressing my hair. I was not scared anymore, nor did I panic. The feeling of disgust overwhelmed me, but my mind was already occupied by my next move. Ivan left with high spirits and said he would see me the following day at the rail station departing for Alushta.

The team was departing for another four-week trip to the small resort place near the Black Sea located on the Crimean Peninsula. I had one more night before the departure and planned my every move for the next day. Because I expected my parents to constantly supervise my movements, I thought of every possible way to escape. The moment came when, in the midst of all preparations, my father asked me to take the garbage out. I did, but instead of coming back, I let my legs carry me away as far as possible until the team's departure time had passed. I spent the day hiding in small, remote places and stood away from crowds, in case my parents decided to pursue me. I waited for night to come, and because it was the first week of July, I knew the time would be late. Eventually, much time had passed and the train had departed from Kharkiv. Now I could come back home without worrying about Ivan.

For the next few days, my parents would not speak to me and my father actually told me that I embarrassed him and my mother in front of my coach. Personally, I did not care about what they thought and spent most of my days at my friend's home or outside hiding until day turned into night. At that time, my parents were fighting a lot and their relationship was crumbling. So my mother asked me to choose between one of them escorting me to Alushta and their divorce. Without hesitation, I said, "Divorce!" To me, our family had fallen apart as soon as I experienced their betrayal. I did not care about what happened next. In the next couple of days, there was not a word spoken between us. Eventually, my mother grabbed me by the arm and took me to the train station without even packing adequate clothes. As she walked holding my hand, she began crying. Her sad facial expression somehow penetrated my soul and I followed her lead. At the train station, she promised to explain why I needed to stay on the team, but only if I would get on the train with her. Being almost twelve years old, this confession really took me off guard and I promised I would go with her. When we sat down, she began her explanation of her problems with my father. She was running out of strength to battle him over childish and unimportant things and thought that if I stayed with Ivan, I would not grow up like him. She told me I was her hope to take care of my younger sisters in the future and Ivan would be more of a father to me than my own biological dad, regardless of how tough Pravilov's methods were. I wanted to extend my heart to her, but I was only a small child and cared about my own fear of experiencing more of Ivan's abuse. There, we made a deal. If Ivan apologized for what he did, although my mother knew nothing about what happened, and promised me no humiliation and no abuse, I would stay on the team. If that did not happen, I would leave instantly and she would take me back home.

This left me some reassurance that she, at least, attempted to be my friend. Upon our arrival, we went to the hotel where the team stayed. Everyone was gone, and the receptionist told us we could find them at the Olympic training complex. When we did find them, my mother grabbed my hand so I would not run away. She walked me toward Ivan and the rest of the team, then suddenly turned and left. By the time I realized what was happening, it was too late. She was already about five yards away when I saw her turning around and walking in the opposite direction. Meanwhile, Ivan instructed nearby players to hold me still and not let go until I calmed down. I began screaming at the top of my lungs for her, but to no avail. I screamed until she vanished from the horizon. Understanding my helpless situation, I abruptly stopped making any noise, astonished over how I could let myself be trapped so easily. Ivan seemed to amuse himself with the image in front of him. Grinning and smiling, he asked me if I had let all the steam out by now. He instructed my "captors" to hold me still for some time until he felt comfortable for them to release my hands. By now, I was simply surprised that no passersby had stopped to inquire about what was happening. They just looked in our direction and carried on with their business. I also realized that I made a fool out of myself, and the humiliation was inevitably upon me. My heart sank and I was again on my own to survive this. That was the moment when I promised myself that I would never rely on my parents again and they could never be fully trusted. I began thinking of ways to escape from there. However, Ivan took that in consideration and made me stay in his room. Whenever the team was free to roam the town, I was assigned to a small group of players who supervised my every move. Although, that was not an order (constant supervision) per se, Ivan never let me be on my own during this trip. Each day passed, and I waited for Ivan's wrath at any moment. I did not trust him for a second. However, to my surprise, he did not touch me one time the entire trip. He would smile without any hidden ideas. He would ask me questions in a normal tone, like I was a human being. He would not instigate other players against me, although a few who were my former slave masters in Uzhgorod could not resist their remarks when no one else was around. They still believed in their superiority over me. When the trip was over, I asked my father to take me to his mother's place to visit. Her village, Andriivka, was about five hours away from Kharkiv, in the Poltava region, and it would have been my perfect sanctuary. In my mind, I could not bear my parents and my coach anymore and chose complete isolation. Knowing my parents could not be trusted, I kept quiet about my intentions and simply waited for the trip to my grandmother's place.

In the meantime, not long before my departure, my parents told me I needed to call my coach. I understood they set it up, but felt I should face my fear regardless. "Do not be a chicken shit," my father responded to my initial refusal. He told me I would be running away from my problems my entire life if I decided to avoid this conversation. My mother pretended to be busy at the moment and showed no attempt to defend me. Believing my father's words, I gathered my strength and went downstairs to call from a public phone. After dialing the number and hearing a few ring tones, the voice on the other end said, "Slushau (I am listening)." I was speechless. Nothing could come out of my mouth. The coach's voice sounded empty and emotionless. *Didn't he ask me to call him?* I thought to myself instantly. For a moment, I thought my parents tricked me but the conversation continued. "What have you to say for yourself?" the coach asked me. "Nothing," I replied, hoping for a quick ending. I was waiting for the usual verbal onslaught, but it never came. Instead, Ivan held a low tone through the entire dialogue. He reminded me of all the great things we did together and accomplished as a team. He spoke of my personal characteristics that, in his view, stood out greatly against other teammates. He told me his perspective on why he picked me on September 9 of 1986 and not others. He asked me if I was willing to throw all that away by walking out on him. *This is not fair*, I thought to myself, *After all the constant abuse and humiliation, this guy is talking about great things we accomplished together.* However, in no time, I was in tears and the conversation lasted for about an hour. Then out of the blue, he asked me to come over. I hesitated and would not respond for a while. *Why does he continue to play with my mind?* I pondered. Ivan would not give in and persisted on me coming to his apartment. Eventually, I gave up and decided to get this over with.

My secret decision had been already made about leaving the team, and now I needed to withstand anything that came at me. I decided to manipulate the situation in any way possible, and lie if necessary until I left for Andriivka. I needed to say all that Ivan wanted to hear and, hopefully soon, I would be out of his grasp. When I arrived, he was in his room lying in bed. He seemed to be asleep, but as soon as I entered, Pravilov opened his eyes and greeted me with a prolonged stare. Then as fast as his eyes opened, they were shut again. Ivan asked me to wake him up in thirty seconds, but I waited for about five minutes until he awoke on his own. The coach frowned, raised his voice, and asked, "What about thirty seconds did you not understand?" My immediate response was that I did not want to disturb him. The game of asking me to wake him up in a few seconds continued for about thirty minutes, until I eventually caught my moment for an escape. Ivan seemed to have fallen asleep, and I slowly crept out of the room. I quietly walked through the hallway and opened the apartment door. When the door was shut behind my back, I wasted no time. The adrenaline rushed through my body. My mind was figuring out different possibilities. This was the seventh floor (if my memory is right), and waiting for an elevator could have cost me precious time. So I galloped down the stairs. I would not run down; I actually leaped halfway over the rails. On the way down, I almost ran over an older man who cursed and threatened to catch me later. When I was out the building, I realized that if I ran the same way I came, I would be an easy target to pursue. So I ran the other way and took an unusual path that Ivan would not expect me to follow. Only when I sat down in one of the public trams and the doors were shut did I exhale in relief. *Now, I am free*, I immediately thought to myself in elation. At home, my parents eagerly awaited my arrival and asked about my confrontation with Ivan. I told them we resolved the problem and there was nothing to worry about. I would take the trip to my grandmother's as a vacation that would clear my mind, which would help me to come back later with new and fresh perspective. They smiled and believed every word, thinking I finally came to my senses. So the next day, feeling good about manipulating my parents and escaping from the terrible coach, I left for my grandmother's place, mentally preparing for a new life.

Some time flew by in Andriivka before I began to revive a little. About one week into my vacation, I had written a letter to my parents resenting my coach and stating I was not willing to come back. I told them this would be my sanctuary and they should not expect me to return. The feeling of freedom did not last for long. One week after my letter, I was outside playing and noticed that my mother had arrived. I knew that the team was leaving shortly for another long trip to Elektrenay in August and this could be another trap. That was enough to make me nervous, so I decided not to come home. I ran away and spent the entire day roaming the streets and crop fields. I slept on benches and spent some time in the pea field. I was scared, but as long as I was away from Pravilov, I could take it with no regrets. A couple of times, I would creep up to my grandmother's house to check if my mother was still there. When away, I never stayed on the road and avoided public places. I preferred country fields that gave me peace and calmness. In those days, a person in the Soviet Union could live well off empty bottles, receiving twenty kopeek for each. Thus, I collected them everywhere I could and submitted them for cash. Eventually, late at night, I walked far away to our relatives' house and without explaining asked to stay there in the mean time. Upon my return to my grandmother's place I declared my serious intentions to stay at her place. Without further questioning, it was enough to convince her, and I hoped that from this point on I began a new life.

When the start of the school year was approaching, my parents wrote me a letter. They pleaded that I had to come back to live with them. They promised me that Ivan would not interrupt my life any longer. They said that I would change schools, because all the players went to the same school (#42) located near Ivan's home. I consulted my grandmother in hopes she would persuade my parents that I could stay with her. Then, I received another letter from them telling me that they were coming and I had to choose while facing them. When they arrived, we made an agreement that as soon as we came back, I would transfer myself to a different school and be completely disassociated from Ivan. I was still reminded that my parents' opinion was against mine, but this time, they allowed me to make a decision for myself. Because my trust had fainted away from them, I gladly transferred the paperwork to another school by myself, without their involvement. That, I thought, was my new beginning. I spent two months in the new environment and loved it. I enjoyed every second of it, because Ivan could no longer control my life and make it miserable. By this time, the end of October approached and my life could not be any better. But one beautiful evening, Ivan came to our home and caught me off guard doing my homework. Up to this day, I do not know if this was a set up or a casual drop in like Ivan claimed. I left it to my parents to tell me later. So, I listened to his plea for my return and many promises that he would stop calling players degrading nicknames. He said he would never raise his hand at any of us again and that he would treat us like human beings. Ivan also reminded me of my escape from his apartment. He told me he understood I did not want to be there and let me go. His casual smile and occasional laughter showed Ivan was rather amused about the situation, but I still accepted his plea.

Within the conversation, I noticed that not once did he apologize for his earlier actions. He always believed in his ways, and the pleas mentioned above provided a good cover for his true self. After our conversation, I was elated about the possibility of playing hockey without physical and mental abuse. I could not wait to get back to my teammates. One of the boys who received Ivan's abuse in Uzhgorod left for his home in Alushta and never came back. The other boy whose parents died stayed and seemed to have no problems in his relationship with the other teammates. I could not believe that his former experiences could be forgotten so fast. When I first arrived for the practice, Ivan welcomed me and told me in front of the team not to be afraid of the same treatment I received earlier in the summer. I was sort of happy, but my mind could never forget the past events. With this in mind, my hockey career with Druzhba-78 resumed and, for better or for worse, I began a new chapter in my life.

Archangelsk

The following several months went by quickly and I enjoyed my return to the team. There were no incidents of physical abuse; there were no humiliating assignments. I was catching up for my lost time and improved significantly in terms of hockey skills. During the winter, our team went to Elektrenay, which held painful and powerful memories. Ivan also decided to show my parents his appreciation for helping him to bring me back and offered to allow my sister to come with us. I was hesitant about it and protested to my parents and her. All they did was laugh and make jokes about what could happen. "This would be a great way for her to see other parts of the country," they said. Without revealing any of the possibilities, I simply responded, "It is her funeral, and I hold no responsibility for anything that happens." But deep underneath, I worried about the possible atrocities. She was only eight (almost nine) at the time and could not comprehend the seriousness of the situation. Despite my protests and personal plea for my sister not to come, she tagged along. So, off we went to the infamous Elektrenay. I fully expected a repeat of the previous nightmare. Although Ivan had kept his word to that moment about no more abuse and humiliation, I suspected he had something new up his sleeve. I mentally prepared for the worst, anticipating that my sister would witness, and perhaps experience, his abuse. I promised myself that if anything happened to her, I would not hesitate to kill him. What would happen to me afterward I cared not; hopefully, it would teach my parents a lesson for their ignorance. Surprisingly, the trip provided only enjoyment and I could not believe that Ivan had a humane side in him. On weekends, he gave players leisure time during the day, and we used it to roam the city. We visited Vilnius, the capital of Lithuania, and Kaunas. It was gorgeous, with numerous historical monuments and buildings, as well as a lot of ice cream that I had never tried before. As a team, we would visit the pool to swim. This was, as I recall, a rare trip that brought no abuse and humiliation upon anyone on the team, at least as far as I know. I was delighted and thought the nightmare was behind us.

The spring was approaching and Ivan planned another trip to Archangelsk located up north, past St. Petersburg. By train, the trip would take two to three days, so to make it quicker, we flew. On the day of our departure, all the parents and players gathered in the city airport a couple of hours ahead of the flight time. To kill time, all the players went to dine and the parents wandered around on their own or sat at different tables. Unfortunately, Ivan positioned himself next to me and, out of the blue, began his jokes about my running away from home the past summer. The laughter from Ivan and the other players penetrated through me like a sharp needle, and I needed to get out. Considering he promised not to mention this to other players and the whole scenario was personal, my anger boiled up again. I lost my appetite and excused myself to the restroom. On my way there, I thought of another trip of torments and decided to run away. I saw that not one parent was anywhere in proximity and the rest of the players were still at the dining table. I also saw a bus approaching the airport station and made a quick run for it. I ran carefully on the icy ground, avoiding slippery spots and allowing my feet to carry me smoothly. The bus stood with open doors, not moving anywhere, and I made my way to it in time. When I seated myself on the opposite side, each second that the doors were open seemed like hours. The bus continued to stay for another minute or so and, finally, the doors were shut. It pulled away from the airport, heading deep into the city.

For a while, I traveled around the city contemplating my next move. Like the past summer, I used bottles to collect some cash and purchase some food. I was in no hurry to return home and loved the feeling of freedom. I also liked the thought of my parents being embarrassed not only in front of Ivan but also all the other parents. I cherished that moment and decided to make them suffer more. I did not return home for three days and, occasionally, would wander near my home in the dark to see what they were doing. Our apartment was located on the second floor of a sixteen-story building, and I could easily see the lights on all night and the shadows moving to and fro. By not returning, I hoped to make a statement to my parents about the seriousness of the situation and that they were perpetuating it. I knew they were panicking based on the lights being on in the middle of the night. I also believed they notified the *milicia* (police), so I tried to never draw any attention to myself. There were other relatives in the city, and I knew where they lived. I thought of contacting them, but not before some time. Just like the past summer, I slept in tiny and hidden spaces where no one could see me. Upon the third night, I contacted my aunt and met her at the rail station near where she lived. Shortly after, my parents came to pick me up. I believed that my message had sunk in somewhat. I would not respond to any of their questions. My trust in them had faded long ago. The incident became an enormous embarrassment to my parents, and I wanted them to be ashamed to even look into the other parents' eyes. Regarding Ivan, I was not concerned, because he could never feel ashamed for his actions.

When the team came back from the trip, Ivan did not show up at my apartment. He probably waited for my parents to contact him, and I do not know if they did. But for one reason or another, I could not feel the presence of fear about possible beatings and humiliating remarks. I simply decided to go to practice and find out the situation for myself. When I entered the locker room, Ivan was smiling and greeted me like I fell out of the sky. Many players began smiling too and some actually loudly laughed. That would not bother me a bit anymore, so I entered farther and stood in front of everyone. Ivan asked me what I had to say for myself. Hesitating to respond, I stood there quietly observing everyone in the locker room. Then the unexpected happened. Laughingly, Ivan asked me how my three days in the city had been. I could not believe he knew this information, but what else could I expect from my parents? After listening to several more remarks about possibly organizing a bum group on the streets, I changed into my hockey gear and moved on.

After all was said and done, I could not help but wonder how despite the trouble I had caused for my parents and Ivan, they were still determined to keep me on the team. I know that my parents were greatly bothered by my behavior, but Ivan saw no problem in it. He would only smile and continue on with his life. From this point on, none of Ivan's surprises and no bad experiences could be considered unexpected. Ivan would be very inventive in his methods and designed new ways to punish his players, but the element of surprise was gone, or so I thought.

Anapa

After the Archangelsk incident, my parents tried to stay away from my relations with Ivan. My last message to them was strong enough not to intervene, so I felt like I won the battle. However, it was too soon to speak of winning the war and I was on a mission to do so. I knew that Ivan would continue his usual behavior and show no deviation in his attitude toward us. I simply took his atrocities for granted and endured every bit of it. My next major fallout with Pravilov happened during our trip the following summer to the small resort in the Crimean Peninsula called Anapa. I was thirteen by then. Ivan again offered to take my sister, so she could experience the Black Sea resort. I was not happy about the possibility and tried to discourage her from coming, but to no avail. She was ten and, to my view, was not ready to experience anything vicious Ivan had to offer. This was my coach's opportunity to really nail my self-esteem. It was one thing to be humiliated and abused in front of my teammates, who knew his ways and expected nothing less, but quite another to become the laughingstock in front of my sister. But seeing her excitement, I went along with it and hoped the trip would be like the last one to Elektrenay, full of joy and excitement.

Our days became routine as soon as we settled in. To my dismay, my sister and I stayed in the same room with Ivan. About a week passed before anything unusual occurred. One day, as a routine procedure, we would go across the monkey bars, but this time, Ivan would not let us stop and demanded to continue until he decided we had enough. After a while, I lost count of how many we did, and each time, I made it to the end. As we continued to exercise on the monkey bars, blisters on my skin had ripped apart and I could no longer bear the pain and hang on. The blood was all over my hands. Other players experienced the same affliction and it seemed that most could no longer make it to the end. More than half the team would either fall off or jump off and go back to the beginning of the line. Eventually, Ivan stopped us and said that, for the last time, we needed to cross the bars to the end and back one at a time.

Those who could not make it were to step aside and then listen for further instructions. Considering that I made it to the end each time before, I thought I could do it for the last time, gathering all my strength. Plus, several players who used to drop down had made it all the way already. Confident in my abilities, I approached the bars and began to walk one grip at a time. My blisters were burning and the bars were slippery from the blood of other players. I made it to the end and now I had to walk back as well. At this point, my palms were also sweating, further weakening my grip. I tried to hang on, understanding that nothing good would happen if I failed. After a few grasps, my hands began to slip and in an attempt to regain my grip, I reached for the next bar with my free hand. That very second, this hand slipped and my grip with the other palm had only fingers touching the bar. That caused me to fall off and I dared not to lift my head up in shame. I could not look at my sister, as the humiliation was unbearable. There were three other players who could not finish the course and stood beside me. When everyone finished, Ivan instructed the team to go to the hotel, change into swimming clothes, and head for the beach. Three of the four that did not make to the end (myself included) were told to remain at the hotel. The fourth was already regarded with such contempt by Ivan that he was no longer acknowledged.

When the team and my sister left, we gathered in one room and discussed what could become of us. We still had another ten days left and each would only bring suffering. After some lengthy consideration, we made a decision to pack our belongings and go home. We knew that Ivan roamed the city during this time and would rarely show up at the beach, so I decided to go to the beach and persuade my sister to come with us. We made an elaborate plan of taking everything with us, and I would personally go to the beach to get my sister. We still needed another trip back for my sister to gather her things, so we moved quickly. I told both of my teammates to wait for me for a certain period of time, hiding in a designated place. If I did not show up by the assigned time, they were to leave without me. When I arrived at the beach, I did not see Ivan in any proximity and my sister was sitting alone. I motioned for her to come over, and she slowly dragged her feet toward me. I asked her if she would come with me. She stared at me and could not understand my question. Then, I asked her again to come with me because I did not have much time. She stood in front of me, puzzled over my words, and asked, "Why?" I could not tell her the reason, fearing she would panic and give my plan away. I tried to be discreet in my responses. I told her that I needed her "yes" or "no" response quickly, and if she decided to stay on the beach, I would go away. With a genuine smile, she turned around and trotted toward the team. I could not waste any time and began to walk away. Soon, I exited the beach and was beyond anyone's view. I accelerated toward the designated hiding place and informed the two players that we were going without her. With all of our belongings intact and leftover money from our parents, we headed for the bus station.

There, without hesitation, we hired a taxi to take us to the train station and split the cost. Upon our arrival, we immediately bought ourselves tickets to Kharkiv. We felt lucky that the train traveled to Kharkiv on the same night and we would not have to wait overnight. Three hours went by before we loaded the train and took off for our home. In the meantime, we alternated the shifts to stand guard near the entrance into the station and agreed to stand our ground if Ivan caught up with us. As soon as we boarded the train, we continued to look out for any signs of our coach, and only after it moved, we relaxed in our seats and discussed our further options. Upon my arrival home, my parents, of course, were stunned. They could not believe I left my sister there alone. My father, as usual, called me a wimp and made no further comment. My mother was worried that something could happen to her. I told them I felt no responsibility about what would happen to my sister, and the whole undertaking was their fault.

When the team arrived nine days later, my sister showed up in full spirits. I asked her if Ivan pursued us and told the team stories about our escape, but she could not respond. Ivan kept her out of the nightly meetings. Two days later, Pravilov showed up at our door to discuss the recent event. Apparently, he was amused with the story and told players that I was the mastermind behind the escape. Convincing him otherwise would be pointless, so I just listened to his remarks and waited for him to leave. No physical abuse happened this time and Ivan actually seemed to be in a good mood. As usual, I returned and began practicing like nothing had happened. A few of the players also saw my escape as very amusing and teased me mercilessly. They constantly reminded me of it for the next several weeks and came up with their own alternatives. That bothered me the least, and my days on the team continued as they were.

International Pee-Wee Tournament, Quebec

Ivan's attitude and his actions toward his players had never improved. I have left out numerous situations in which Ivan found something humiliating to laugh about or exhibited random, short outbursts. My coach made a gradual transformation from a somewhat rational tyrant to a despicable monster. Eventually, his abuse and harassment became more random and unpredictable. Ivan did it because he felt like it. He slowly began distrusting anyone surrounding the team, as well as the players on it. He became more violent and instances of his brutal approach had increased significantly. His smoking habits had escalated. Ivan could easily go through two or more packs a day, and his car reeked with the smell. Pravilov's drinking habits had followed the same route. He would also never miss an opportunity to point out someone's habits and physical traits that could be easily ridiculed and made fun of. For example, for six months, I had to wear orthodontics to straighten my teeth. They were very uncomfortable and big. Soon, my coach picked up on this and began calling me a vampire and other names. To some, it might not sound harsh, but when it came out of his mouth, the words were tortuous. Nevertheless, the life on Druzhba-78 continued and after one of our trips to Czechoslovakia, we received an invitation to Canada to play in the prestigious international tournament in Quebec. The tournament was scheduled for the coming winter in February of 1992.

Upon our arrival, we began playing many exhibition games and before our first official tournament game at the Coliseum, former home of the Quebec Nordics, our team had made a name for itself. We won most of the games with a significant gap in score and dazzled spectators with speed and skill. We eventually won the tournament and invitations from many North American hockey clubs started pouring in. The tournament appeared to be the beginning of Ivan's rise as a "genius" instructor and coach in many people's eyes. Druzhba-78 was recognized on a wider scale, and now Ivan had a window into the world of opportunities. Soon after the tournament, we visited several other places like Toronto and Washington, D.C. Our arrival to Ukraine was delayed a couple of months, and everywhere we went, the spectators watched our performances with awe. Little did they know at what cost this "well-disciplined" group of children played the game.

Prior to the tournament, Ivan was able to persuade a few players from other areas of the former Soviet Union to join our team for this trip. One of them was from Ufa, Kazakhstan, and he became my roommate throughout his experience on Druzhba-78. Not long had gone by before he began witnessing odd things. Ivan would ask him questions that were very personal and start conversations on seemingly irrelevant topics. At one point, my roommate asked me if Ivan was out of his mind. The questions he was asked were, "Do you love your parents?" or "Who do you love the most?" My roommate was laughing at the conversations and was surprised we could endure our coach for such a long time. Back then, I realized that Ivan purposefully made the two of us stay with him in Washington, D.C. while other players were billeted by other families. He probed every new player for his potential to be loyal and submissive, and my roommate was no exception. Unlike many other newcomers, this player would not bend under Ivan's prolonged questionnaire and, I believe, would confront Pravilov with questions of his own. Although my roommate was an excellent hockey player and any team would have loved having him, for some reason, he could not fit into our group. Several times he asked me why I was afraid of my coach and defended him. He thought our subordination toward him was ridiculous and would probably smile at the thought of sticking around any longer.

When we arrived to Kharkiv, Ivan invited him one more time to his apartment, likely for another mind game conversation. But I guess there were no compromises, and my roommate left for his hometown shortly thereafter. After his departure, Ivan explained to us that my former roommate could not be apart from his family and was eager to see his parents and younger brothers again. However, from the beginning, I suspected their relationship would not last because Ivan could not bear open-minded and self-assured individuals. Personally, I cannot recall at any point of my experience with Ivan his capacity to praise someone's abilities. If you performed well, he would simply be quiet. During the rare times that Ivan showed positive emotion, I did not trust him. If our performance was not up to his standards, he would unleash his fury. In addition to all the other abuses and ridicules we endured, he would never forget to remind his players of how worthless they were. This mind-set persisted throughout all of my ten years in Druzhba-78, and I could not recover from such constant remarks for a long time. I had heard these comments for so long, I believed them to be true. In any case, Ivan's relationship with my former roommate was one of the rare situations when Pravilov could not subdue someone's mind and soul.

Pee-Wee Tournament, Quebec, Canada - February 1992

Pee Wee Pro   BARANKOVSKIY A. N.

TOURNOI INTERNATIONAL DE HOCKEY
PEE WEE DE QUÉBEC   Pee Wee Pro

Pee Wee Pro   BULIGA ANATOLY V.

TOURNOI INTERNATIONAL DE HOCKEY
PEE WEE DE QUÉBEC

Pee Wee Pro

Pee Wee Pro   DRIGULAS SERGEI V.

TOURNOI INTERNATIONAL DE HOCKEY
PEE WEE DE QUÉBEC

Pee Wee Pro

Pee Wee Pro KALMIKOV K. SERGEI

  TOURNOI INTERNATIONAL DE HOCKEY Pee Wee Pro
PEE WEE DE QUÉBEC

Pee Wee Pro   KLUCHKO DMITRY I.

TOURNOI INTERNATIONAL DE HOCKEY
PEE WEE DE QUÉBEC

Pee Wee Pro

Pee Wee Pro   LUPANDIN ANDREI N.

K H A R K O V

K H A R K O V

**TOURNOI INTERNATIONAL DE HOCKEY
PEE WEE DE QUÉBEC**

Pee Wee Pro

Pee Wee Pro   MARAKHOVSKIY R. N.

K H A R K O V

K H A R K O V

TOURNOI INTERNATIONAL DE HOCKEY
PEE WEE DE QUÉBEC

Pee Wee Pro

Pee Wee Pro   PANASENKO OIEG V.

K H A R K O V

K H A R K O V

TOURNOI INTERNATIONAL DE HOCKEY
PEE WEE DE QUÉBEC

Pee Wee Pro

Pee Wee Pro PRAVILOV IVAN N.

TOURNOI INTERNATIONAL DE HOCKEY
PEE WEE DE QUÉBEC

Pee Wee Pro

Pee Wee Pro   RAZIN GENNADY V.

KHARKOV

KHARKOV

TOURNOI INTERNATIONAL DE HOCKEY
PEE WEE DE QUÉBEC

Pee Wee Pro

Pee Wee Pro ROMANUKHA D. M.

TOURNOI INTERNATIONAL DE HOCKEY
PEE WEE DE QUÉBEC Pee Wee Pro

Pee Wee Pro   SEROV VLADISLAV A.

TOURNOI INTERNATIONAL DE HOCKEY
PEE WEE DE QUÉBEC   Pee Wee Pro

Pee Wee Pro   SHIRYAEV DENIS A.

TOURNOI INTERNATIONAL DE HOCKEY
PEE WEE DE QUÉBEC   Pee Wee Pro

Pee Wee Pro   SIRENKO DMITRY B.

TOURNOI INTERNATIONAL DE HOCKEY
PEE WEE DE QUÉBEC   Pee Wee Pro

Pee Wee Pro   STARCHENKO M. N.

K H A R K O V

V O K R A H K

#9

TOURNOI INTERNATIONAL DE HOCKEY
PEE WEE DE QUÉBEC

Pee Wee Pro

TOURNOI INTERNATIONAL DE HOCKEY
PEE WEE DE QUÉBEC

Pee Wee Pro　　YAKUSHIN DMITRY V.

TOURNOI INTERNATIONAL DE HOCKEY
PEE WEE DE QUÉBEC

Pee Wee Pro

Pee Wee Pro ZUBRUS DAINUS G.

TOURNOI INTERNATIONAL DE HOCKEY
PEE WEE DE QUÉBEC

Pee Wee Pro

Pee Wee Pro   ZUZIN ANDREI Y.

K H A R K O V

KHARKOV

TOURNOI INTERNATIONAL DE HOCKEY
PEE WEE DE QUÉBEC   Pee Wee Pro

Summer, 1992

After our first visit to North America, as I mentioned earlier, many hockey clubs began inviting Druzhba-78 to come over and play a series of games. As soon as we returned to Ukraine, Ivan began planning another trip in the summer. Although not much ridicule and abuse happened during our recent voyage, nothing could be certain with Ivan.

This time, Ivan persuaded a new player from Kiev to join our team and thought the trip would be a good test for him. The player stayed with my family in Kharkiv before our departure for North America and we became good friends. Throughout the trip, though, we were separated and stayed with other roommates. The player could never blend in, and perhaps confronted Ivan during one of his mind tests. One way or another, I felt he was doomed to leave and Ivan wasted no time sending him home in the middle of our trip. Only this player and Ivan know what actually happened.

During most of our trip we visited Toronto, Canada, and many families were willing to take us in. Initially, I stayed with two other boys with one of the Italian families in Richmond Hill near Toronto. All was well, until one day, Ivan decided to visit us for dinner. While all of us played video games downstairs, Ivan came into our room and found my roommate's diary lying on the bed. He began looking through the pages and found disturbing information that could probably jeopardize his status in the future. Because the player had only recently joined our team (he came from Kiev just before the Quebec tournament earlier that year), he could not fully understand the magnitude of Ivan's true self. As a result, he would write the experiences at face value and had no second thoughts about the potential consequences. Our coach called him into the room and spent a significant amount of time behind closed doors. What went on I do not know, but after the conversation, the player became Ivan's prime target for the rest of the trip and all coming years on the team. Soon, Ivan notified the rest of the team about my roommate's diary and blamed his desire for fame. However, from the very beginning, I felt Ivan was covering what the player truly wrote and made him feel worthless to discourage further memoirs. He chastised the player with verbal abuse and alienated him from the rest of the team. I still do not understand why he continued to stay on Druzhba. However, the same question could be asked of any of the players, considering the horrors they each experienced.

After several weeks, Druzhba-78 was transferred to stay with Ukrainian families. As before, Ivan visited the family another teammate and I billeted with and stayed for dinner. When everyone was done eating, the family's son, our coach, and my roommate and I went to the basement to play video games. Ivan would sit on the side, quietly observing every one of our moves. After several minutes of dead and intense silence, the family's son became very uncomfortable and began asking us some questions, probably wanting to elevate our spirits and cheer us up. That did not go well, as both of us hoped the other would respond and eventually ended up staring at the computer game in silence. The family's son probably noticed the fright on our faces and ceased his questions. He also became quiet, but probably wondered what suddenly happened that forced us to shut up completely. In about twenty to twenty-five minutes, Pravilov decided to leave and abruptly went upstairs to say his farewell to the hosts. We walked him to the door. After his departure, we returned downstairs to continue the computer games. This time, without Ivan's constant supervision, we were able to relax and respond to the questions. That behavior did not go unnoticed and the hosts' son asked us why we were so afraid of our coach. He told us he felt Ivan controlled each of our movements with a remote controller and only let us answer questions with his approval. We, of course, would only defend him, explaining that none of us were scared. The son would not really argue but stated what he witnessed and that we could not convince him otherwise. Such instances occurred throughout each visit to North America, and many witnessed our fright upon our proximity with the coach. Most would look the other way, not wanting to deal with our problems; some would only ask the players questions and be satisfied with our positive responses, and very few would actually confront Ivan about what happened on the team in the background. Because Ivan could always come up with an excuse, for one reason or another, they would back away and pursue the issue no further. In some cases, Ivan would turn his fury against them and blame them for ruining our team's chemistry. Eventually, he would instruct some of us to support him and talk back to those who attempted to portray our team (our coach) in a negative light.

During this trip, Pravilov discovered that one of the players excelled in the English language and decided to officially appoint him his translator. The player came earlier from another city (Doneck) and, although he witnessed Ivan's brutal approach, stuck around. In any case, Pravilov's translator would be at his side at all times and this boy became the victim of some of Ivan's worst beatings. He followed Ivan's every move and was under constant supervision. Because of the coach's very short temper, the translator was expected not to make any mistakes. That meant the boy would receive punishment for each of his stumbles and became his punching bag for the rest of his association with Druzhba-78. Recalling my earlier experiences with Ivan, I had thought nothing could top the Uzhgorod beatings and verbal abuses. But seeing this teammate at Ivan's side every second made me feel very sorry for him. Sometimes, his cheeks would be swollen the size of a grown person's fist. His eyes cried out "I need some sleep and peace from this monster. I need to get away from him." They were so dark that I could not distinguish the reasons. Were they from beatings or a lack of sleep? After a while, his breath became unbearable to bystanders. His lips would be swollen and gums bled. Ivan instructed him to brush his teeth every three hours, but even that could not take the stench away. With every consecutive trip to North America, the boy became a victim of harsher punishments. During the following trips (the team would travel for two or three months every winter and summer until the summer of 1995), he would appear with bruises all over his body. Some of them were the size of my palm and few expanded throughout the whole side of his leg. I could only imagine the types of abuses he received from Pravilov, and I do not remember him complaining even once. But nothing could be more disturbing than the fact that Ivan got away with such atrocities. The boy would always smile and say that he either had gotten into a fight or received a vicious hit during a game. Ivan must have come up with some elaborate excuses himself, because when faced with the questions and inquiring stares from outsiders, most just looked the other way.

This boy left for his hometown of Doneck in the fall of 1993, after four trips to North America. Upon his departure, he left Ivan a letter explaining his reasons and blamed his own weak will for not being able to stick around any longer. He thanked Ivan for all the good things he had done for him and for making him a stronger person. I have no idea what these "good" things were that he wrote about. Nevertheless, as Ivan read the letter to the rest of the team after one of our practices, he could not help but amuse himself. He laughed at some of the quotes and said, "Jews never stick around when the hard times come." Such remarks came from our coach often toward many players, and this was no different. The boy was probably so frightened of Ivan's reprimands that he left the letter with his billet family without confronting him. I could not blame him for this resolution, as my earlier experience proved that Ivan would take these instances personally. If he did not escape, Pravilov would only make his life worse.

"Golubie" and "Pederasti"

Truthfully, my experiences on Druzhba 78, while horrific, are only mild when compared to those of some of my teammates. The humiliation, torture, and abuse they suffered at Ivan's hands are unthinkable. At fourteen and fifteen years old, our coach's mind games and manipulation led to intense feelings of inferiority and worthlessness. Eventually, Ivan began calling certain players Golubie and Pederasti. "*Goluboy*" is a Russian word that is literally translated as "light blue." Informally, the term, or slang if you will, is directly pointed at an individual of homosexual orientation in a derogatory way. In North American culture, it would be the same as "faggot." "*Golubie*" is simply a plural form that means "faggots." "*Pederast*," on the other hand, is an international word that is common to several languages. It is an adult or an adolescent who engages in a (usually erotic) relationship with a younger boy outside his immediate family. In English, the term would be "pedophile." Just like *golubie*, *pederasti* is simply the Russian plural form. Ivan used these words constantly as insults toward specific players.

At first, this particular humiliation seemed limited to name-calling alone. But soon, Ivan began to push this subject further. He would recount details about situations to which the players in focus had supposedly confessed. He would make a mockery out of them, making them stand in front of everyone repeating their "*goluboy*" stories that Ivan claimed to have recently squeezed out of them in private. He creatively forced those boys to "confess" who they liked on our team and what they wanted to do with them. At first, I could not comprehend the seriousness of the situation. But soon, I witnessed and understood that Ivan would not stop at anything. He demanded details, and especially dirty ones. Each consecutive story made our coach more ecstatic, and he constantly demanded more and more. There was no end to his thirst. Eventually, after the humiliation would come to an end for that day, everyone else would be instructed to go home, while the player in focus stayed behind locked doors with Ivan. Only those victims know exactly what happened next.

On countless occasions, I asked myself how Pravilov could be capable of such acts. With each progression, I could not imagine that things could get any worse. He would continue terrorizing us until we had no strength left to resist. His constant pressure upon our minds and bodies was exhausting. I thought the Uzhgorod experience was the epitome of evil, yet witnessing the humiliation some of my teammates endured made me feel lucky I was only beaten, although almost to death. The humiliated players in the middle of the locker room probably thought the same thing. No one wanted to be called "*goluboy*" or "*pederast*," and especially when our coach literally accused them of being one. To add salt to the wound, he smiled and laughed profusely during such sessions, implying that he could do anything to us and get away with it. Sometimes he created new stories for his own entertainment and made the boys play them out in front of the entire team. To my disgust, a few players actually laughed at what was happening in front of them. Ivan fed off it, constantly creating new situations. His hunger was never satisfied. Two such instances continue to stand out in my mind.

During one of our meetings (Ivan loved his "meetings"!), one of the players was "instructed" to demonstrate and explain in detail all aspects of his act. Pravilov claimed he had already seen it and heard all the details in private. Now it was our turn to witness, with our coach present in the room. The player in focus was told to demonstrate and explain as he went how he satisfied himself when the urge for other boys would be unbearable. As usual, I would sit there frozen, initially staring at what was transpiring in front of my eyes. I felt disgusted and, at the same time, furious at my coach. His sick games have gone overboard. My blood boiled, but I felt scared and helpless. The boy in front of us lay on the floor on his back. He lifted his legs straight in the air holding them together and pushed his torso off the floor over his head, with his buttocks against the wall for balance. Keeping the body extended straight up (in an inverted position) and providing additional support with his elbows and the back of his head, the player bent his legs 90 degrees.

At first, I thought this was some kind of new and bizarre exercise that Ivan came up with. But to my dismay, what happened next sent chills throughout my body. The boy extended both of his hands underneath his shorts with one hand holding his penis and the other pushing the waistband out to create room. In no time, the first hand started moving back and forth. As this was happening, Ivan demanded a clear explanation of every step of the way. He seemed to be in his glory and enjoyed our mournful expressions. Moreover, the player was told to demonstrate how much he enjoyed the act. For that, he was to intermittently moan and sound orgasmic. All this was too much for my eyes and ears. But if I covered them, I feared Pravilov would unleash his wrath against me. So I continued looking in the same direction and hearing the sounds. Others did the same. For a moment, I was able to glance at my teammates and see their gloomy faces. Some tried to escape the view by staring through the scene into a far wall. Their bodies looked petrified and glued to where they sat. Some looked dead, with no expression at all. Some made an attempt to shift a bit, but this only provided our coach an incentive for ridicule and questions like "You are so excited that you can't even sit still, aren't you?" Meanwhile, the player in focus continued his "exercise." Ivan demanded an explanation of what exactly needed to be achieved. The player began by opening his mouth. The goal was to masturbate until an orgasm arrived, after which the semen would shoot straight into his mouth.

This continued for some time. Each minute seemed to drag forever. I sat there in anticipation for it to be over. *Is Ivan really this crazy?* I thought to myself. I actually felt nauseous and light-headed. I understood that showing weakness would provoke Pravilov's impulses. He could make me his next target. So I held my ground, not giving my coach any reason to redirect his attention toward me. I had to be strong to survive this madness. The tension in the room was high. No one dared to make a sound or move. The only noise came from the player on the floor. After about ten minutes, the boy told Pravilov he could not finish, to which he heard Ivan respond, "*Prodolzhay, Goluboy* (Continue, Faggot)." Then Ivan used another boy as a reference, saying that the "*goluboy*" should imagine that the other player was fondling him. That brought some attention to the player he referred to, and his face turned pale. I felt sorry for him, but could not completely deviate my attention away from the main event. I needed to focus on something else, but nothing would pop into my mind. I felt scared and enraged simultaneously. The player on the floor pled several more times that he could not finish, but our coach ordered him not to stop.

About another ten minutes passed when our coach suddenly hit a player, sitting close to him, on the back, saying, "Would you like to join him? You never know, you might like it." Pravilov thought it was funny, having a big grin on his face. He definitely enjoyed this. The entire twenty minutes, not a player spoke a word except the one on the floor pleading and by now exhausted from the position he was in. Everyone waited for it to be over, but not our coach. The amusement was too great to pass on. He giddily encouraged the player to masturbate faster and other times to go slower, sounding confident in his directions. At one point, I thought Ivan came up with the "exercise" based on his own experience, considering the amount of direction he gave. *He knows a lot about it*, I thought to myself, but kept quiet.

Eventually, Ivan's patience ran out. He instructed the boy to stop the "exercise." The boy was exhausted and sore from the position and simply just leaned against the wall sitting on the floor. Then he heard, "That's okay, you will perform better next time. You will teach your friends how to be a faggot." The meeting continued for another hour or so with a one-way communication from our wonderful coach. He preached morality and honesty, sometimes pointing his finger at the player sitting on the floor. He made him feel worthless and not deserving of any compassion. He portrayed him as inhuman. This event, I believed, showed the magnitude of our coach's twisted mind. But the next event I will describe overshadowed any other experience, including the one illustrated above.

It all began during our training camp at Severodoneck, sometime after the above incident. During this four-week trip, Ivan picked on his target, designing different ways to humiliate and abuse him. The build up toward the eventual episode was unbearable for the boy in focus. He had endured enough already and I could not believe that Pravilov still was not satisfied. The boy, of course, was secluded from the rest of the team. He kept his distance whenever and wherever we went. He was endlessly bombarded by Ivan's insults. They included jokes of a homosexual nature, as well as few acts of role-playing in front of the entire squad. By now, I believe, the player had become used to such insults and simply blocked everything out of his mind. He followed "instructions" on autopilot. When the final incident occurred, it struck me more than anything before.

During one of the practices, everyone went on the ice. The player mentioned above stayed behind. He was told to remain there until instructed otherwise. We skated for two hours without Ivan's presence, not knowing exactly what was taking place in the locker room, but expecting it was likely horrific. For our own safety, we minded our own business, hoping it would end soon. In any case, the practice time ran out and we were on our way back. Upon entrance, nothing seemed unusual. The player sat in the corner in his seat, while Ivan stood across the room with a hockey stick in his hand. At first I thought that many stick massages had resolved our coach's twisted mind, but I was wrong. Although I did not doubt that many rounds of stick massage had been issued, something else had happened. With a wide grin on his face, our coach directed everyone's attention to the knob of the hockey stick he held in his hands. I noticed some brown residue on it about one inch long. Ivan asked one of the players standing close to him if he wanted to know what happened in the locker room while everyone was on the ice. I did not believe anyone desired any knowledge, but our coach persisted. Without waiting for anyone's response he proudly said that the residue on the hockey stick's knob was from the player sitting in the corner. We all looked at him, but our teammate would not look up. He stared at the floor, with some tears in his eyes. I immediately suspected that Ivan was the one shoving the stick, but could not prove anything as the incident happened behind locked doors. Meanwhile, Ivan went on with his proud moment. He spoke of it with such elation that one would think this was his greatest accomplishment of the entire trip. "Look how far this stick got into the player's butt hole," he excitedly told us. "I would not have ever believed if I never saw it with my own eyes." Then Pravilov asked another player if he would like to lick the residue off the knob, pushing it into his face. By doing so, he repeatedly smacked his lips, as one might do when presented with a tasty dessert. The boy who faced this knob turned his face away, but Ivan kept extending it forward, almost sticking the knob into his mouth. That continued for a minute or so until our coach had enough. He pulled the hockey stick away and, moving his attention directly at the player in the corner, said, "To be continued. Next time, we will go for a record." We all changed into our clothes and moved on without a sound. I believed the scene was too much to endure and think about, so we never, at least to my knowledge, bothered to ask what exactly happened.

At the moment, many feelings had rushed through my mind. My blood was boiling, but I also felt pathetically hopeless and helpless. I just witnessed something I had never thought was possible, even for Ivan, and still had no strength to stand up to the tyrant. I was scared and sympathetic for my team-mate. The memories of Uzhgorod and the captain's vote had bothered me a lot, but this was beyond my own understanding. The boys who Ivan called "*golubie*" and "*pederasti*" had endured an enormous humiliation and abuse in front of our eyes. However, that was only a small fraction of their story. Behind the scenes and closed doors, there was even greater harassment, abuse, and torture. Ivan stopped at nothing and made it clear that his role on our team was similar to those of Stalin's and Hitler's in their time and place. He used his devious methods to suppress each individual's self-confidence. He pun-ished us ferociously for having any thought or opinion of our own. He made us robots and slaves of his will. I remembered personal feelings of humiliation after Ivan picked me as his target for abuse. But this was different. I would rather be beaten, I thought to myself, than to experience what I had just wit-nessed. The body could heal; the mind could not. Those players have to live with these experiences their entire lives and cope with psychological conse-quences that will not be easy to overcome. With it, Pravilov crossed all bound-aries of human morals and ethics, all the while proclaiming his righteous behavior toward "his" children. The two instances described above are merely singular examples of the extensive sexual harassment and abuse Ivan used on the boys he called *golubie* and *pederasti*. Even in the Soviet system of oppres-sion, persecution, and punishment, such methods would not be accepted. Ivan used the system against us to ultimately empower himself. He ruled us without much resistance, portraying himself as the Stalin of his time.

Detroit Scramble

Between the second and fourth trips (summer of 1992 and summer of 1993) to North America, our team had experienced another of Ivan's experiments, although similar incidents happened many times before. During our short trip to Detroit after visiting Chicago, our team was invited to play against several local teams. After the first game, which happened to be our first loss of the campaign, Ivan spent about an hour lecturing us in the locker room behind locked doors. For the entire hour, not a single soul had made a sound. Our coach was enraged by our performance and promised us a night to remember. When we returned to our hotel, Ivan immediately called everyone to his room for a team meeting. All prepared for the worst, as the mood on our coach's face was not pleasant, to say the least.

Sitting in the back corner of the room and smoking what appeared to be his second or third pack of cigarettes, Pravilov spent a few moments observing each one of us standing and sitting before him with our heads down. All of us fought for the space farthest from him and no one wanted to be positioned in the foreground. About three minutes went by before our coach broke the dead silence. "Nu chto druzhbani, chto budem delat'? (So, my friends, what are we going to do now?)" The question was more of a statement, signifying that this would be a long night. No one volunteered to respond as we all sat and stood there in silence, avoiding Ivan's glaring eyes. The smoke had filled the room and the coach began lighting his second cigarette. That very instant, Ivan called out one of the players by his nickname (by that time, almost no player was called by his real name) and asked him the same question. The response was, "You should punish us." A sadistic smirk appeared on Ivan's face and in a sarcastic tone he exclaimed, "Do I deserve to mar my hands over your and everyone else's face?" I could sense the dilemma in the player's mind. He hesitated to answer, probably pondering over the probable consequences of his possible response. So the player resorted to a neutral position and said, "I do not know." Ivan never liked these answers and became furious. "I tell you

71

what," he said. "Today, you must decide on who deserves the most punishment, but you will be the one executing it." As soon as Ivan spoke those words, I thought in my mind that this could be the return of the old "Temnaya" days. One player would probably be picked to suffer the consequences and others would be instructed to deliver the "execution." I hoped my name would not be announced and held my breath. Another player's name was called upon. I exhaled with relief but felt sorry for my poor teammate.

Referring to the "executioner," Ivan said that this was his chance to make the other pay for his sins. "What should I do?" the executioner asked. Our coach seemed to find this entertaining and told him to use his imagination. "Be creative and demonstrate how much you hate him," he said. The other player waited for the onslaught, but it had not come. The executioner stood there petrified. Becoming impatient, Ivan asked him what was he waiting for. Dead silence covered the room, so now Ivan asked the player who was to be punished to show the executioner how the punishment was supposed to be done. I could see the hesitation, but he delivered a slow punch on the face. Ivan said that it did not count because he knew how a punch should be delivered when true hatred was behind it. Consequently, there was a faster swing and a louder landing of the fist. This time, Ivan was more satisfied but still demanded a harder blow. Only this time, he asked the new executioner not to hit the victim's face. In his words, he did not want to spoil his cute face. "He would probably tell on every one, if someone inquired about it," he said. But in my mind, I knew Ivan would not respond to any accusations and would not get in trouble. Nevertheless, the other player provided a fast blow into the executioner's stomach. The executioner's face turned red and the punch forced him to bend over. In response, Ivan asked him if he hated the other yet. I do not believe the hate was directed at the other player, but the survival instinct kicked in and several hard blows followed. Now, I saw a complete turnaround and the executioner wildly threw some punches without remorse. Meanwhile, Ivan remained in the back corner of the room. A big smile would not leave his face, an expression I was so familiar with. At this point, my hatred toward Ivan reached new heights, and I could not believe that someone would actually enjoy this spectacle. After several punches, Pravilov turned his attention back to the other player and asked him how he could take this beating without retaliating in return. This encouragement fostered the other player to fight back and a fierce struggle ensued in front of us. Because everyone moved a few paces back, a big portion of the room had cleared. Both players wrestled each other for a few short moments until the other player got the better of the executioner. The executioner was on the bed while the other climbed on top of him, holding his arms still. The next moment, I saw the other player locking the executioner's arms with his knees and strangling him with his hands. The rest of us stood motionless, not making a single attempt to help either party. We observed the spectacle without emotions, providing no reason to be picked next by our coach. Shortly, the situation had gotten so out of hand that Ivan yelled out to the three closest players to pull the other player off the executioner. "Wow!" our coach exclaimed. "You two really hate each other. Why would you say otherwise beforehand? This means you were lying."

I thought the demonstration had ended. Ivan usually completed his entertainment sessions after a single example and continued lecturing on how worthless our lives were. But as I found out soon enough, this was only a warm up. Although I learned not to take anything for granted when dealing with him, I had not expected the next move. Ivan asked the executioner if he thought there were others in need of a punishment. Looking over the rest of the players, the executioner called out three more teammates. They reluctantly moved forward and now stood facing Ivan in the middle of the room. Pravilov wasted no time and commented that they were to receive a punishment from the executioner. Our coach directed them to face their punisher standing in one row. As soon as they obeyed the command, Ivan instructed the punisher to execute the judgment. Taking it as a direct order, he began throwing his fist into the others' stomachs. The punches were not hard, and Ivan instructed him to repeat the blows. If he performed his second set of blows in a similar fashion, he was to receive his own punishment later. Not wanting to be the recipient, he executed as instructed and delivered hard swings.

What came next was a predictable move on our coach's behalf (at least to me). He turned his attention on the executioner and began the familiar mind games. My teammate felt trapped, as I saw his confused look and a sense of helplessness. However, that look lasted only a few seconds. I believe he knew those games too well not to recognize the pattern. In a quick moment, the perplexed look had changed to anger, and I think he could not believe he allowed himself to be trapped into the web of Ivan's games. The sensation was very familiar to me, as I had experienced those moments with our coach many times over the years. Now I only hoped the damage would be minimal and my name would not be drawn into this mess. Nevertheless, Ivan asked the executioner, "Why did you tell me before that you loved your teammates and were ready to do anything to defend them?" He further continued, "That, as I saw, was not what I would call love." It was one of those moments when we knew that if we did not perform what Ivan demanded, we would suffer dire consequences later. But if we executed his commands, Pravilov would find a way to turn it against us. So the player stood there speechless and motionless, afraid to make any wrong moves or say wrong things. Ivan would not stop his charade and resumed what he started. In reference to the executioner, he directed his speech to the rest of the team. "Look at your teammate right now," our coach spoke in a hissing tone. "Just moments ago, he swore his love to every one of you and told you that nothing could change his mind. However, when facing dire consequences, his fright of being punished himself turned him into a traitor. How could anyone go to war alongside him, when he could turn his own mother in just to stay alive? Now, he must suffer the consequences for his betrayal to the rest of the team."

Based on my experience, I understood the significance of those words. The player had no way out of it. Arguing would only make things worse, and all the player could do was receive what was coming and get on with it. Ivan redirected his focus on the four players whose names were called upon earlier. He instructed them to teach the executioner a lesson for his betrayal and show their utmost hatred toward him. In a few seconds, they unleashed their fury and began hitting and punching him anywhere but the face, as instructed. This lasted for about a minute, until Pravilov decided it was enough. When each of them got up, Ivan did something unexpected. He changed his course of direction and asked one of the four players executing the punishment why he hated the executioner so much. The response was obvious: "Because he betrayed us." The next second, Ivan started laughing, with a cigarette in his hand and the smoke spreading throughout. "How did he actually betray you?" Ivan asked. I realized that now, Ivan had turned his mind game against this player and he could become the next recipient of the punishment. Regardless of his answer, our coach would always find a way to make it happen. So, as I expected, the player gave him the explanation of the recent scenario and told him that betrayal should not be overlooked. Continuing his intermittent laughs, Ivan asked, "So, now you will listen to each of my words that I speak?" Not waiting for a response, he added, "Are you blaming me for what you did to him?" pointing his finger at the recipient of the recent beating. I could see that this player had enough experience with Ivan's games and understood the inevitability of his doom. He stood there quietly, just waiting and accepting his fate.

The executioner stood by this player and was instructed to beat him up for what the player did to him. To make things more interesting for his own amusement, our coach told the player not to retaliate. The executioner let a few blows fly in the stomach and the sides. In a few moments, Ivan instructed the other three standing by to join the executioner. Some blows were so hard that I could not imagine the pain that the recipient suffered. I tilted my head down and tried not to see what was happening. Luckily, Ivan either did not notice, being completely focused on the spectacle in front of him, or showed no interest in bringing up the fact. Turning my eyes away did not help; I could still hear the thumping sound from the blows and just held my breath, hoping no one would end up dead after this night. Pravilov let this continue for about two minutes and stopped when one of the four "punishers" had almost choked the recipient to death. Still smoking his cigarette and smiling like nothing had happened, he continued his mind games. The "meeting" went on for a while and one or two more players from that crowd became the unfortunate recipients of this madness.

This summit had ended like many others. He began analyzing the situation and told us how all of us hated one another. "You cannot hide that hatred from me and better let it out now in front of the teammates," he would comment. He told us that our recent game demonstrated what we witnessed in front of us here. He made a comment that we played the game exactly like we behaved in front of him in this room, and this was just an example how every one of us was able to turn against one another in a moment's notice. He spoke of the recent events in such a calm manner that I probably would not believe it had happened if I did not witness it. *Could anyone actually believe this story? I thought, standing there and listening to him preach.* Does this monster believe he could get away with this tyranny? But again, he was able to weasel out of all previous situations without a scratch, and this would be no different.

Ivan demonstrated his true intention of controlling not only our behavior but also our thoughts about each other. He turned several meetings into a brawl and alienated us for his own power. He understood that with hatred toward each other, we would have no trust toward one another. Without trust, we would only worry about our own fates, instead of uniting against him. The instances described above happened in many trips in the past since the beginning and increased with each trip to North America. Ivan saw no other option in order to maintain his rule over us. Those who rebelled could not stay on the team for long, as Pravilov would always resort to alienation tactics and give the rebels no other alternative. Ivan told us that he would never throw anyone off the team, but his tactics would force them out, given there was no hope in fighting back.

Hotel in New York, Pizza Story

When I barely turned fifteen, during our fourth trip to North America in the summer of 1993, the team could not find a place to go and temporarily landed in one of the hotels in New York City for two nights. As soon as the team had gotten into the hotel and the players were placed in their rooms, we received one pizza per room. Because I carried the pizza in for our room, I was also picked to ask our coach if we could eat it. After a tedious day and night in New York City, spending most of the time waiting at the subway station and having nothing to eat, everyone was very hungry. For that reason, we were eager to devour the meal in front of us; however, eating it without Ivan's permission would mean harsh punishment. So, I went out in the hallway where Ivan held a conversation with our temporary guide about the team's next move. I knew better than to interrupt, for there could be dire consequences. Therefore, I waited for about three minutes until both of them began walking away. Knowing that this could be my only chance for a while to ask the question, I recited the words, "Ivan Nikolaevich, could we eat the pizza?" The question was repeated three times before a response followed. The coach just waived his arm and said, "Do whatever you want with it." Upon my arrival into the room, I told the other three roommates that we could eat, assuming that Pravilov's response meant just that. One of the boys asked me the coach's exact words, to which I repeated his response to the letter. My teammates pondered a little and one of them doubted my assumption. I reassured him of my decision and, eventually, all took their shares to eat. A few minutes went by before I began doubting myself, but by now, the pizza was gone and the time could not be turned back. My decision would cost all four of us dearly.

A couple of hours had gone by before Ivan entered our room. The pizza had been eaten and he saw the empty box. Our coach grabbed and threw it at one of us. We all jumped up, preparing for the worst. By staring at one of the boys, he growled, "Who allowed you to eat it?" Because another player received the maddening stare, he felt obligated to respond and said what I had told him earlier. Ivan was enraged and apparently could not hear the player's words that I was the one who told them they were allowed to eat. He approached him and, without hesitation, landed a couple of fists on his face. The player fell on the floor but got up quickly, knowing that lying down would infuriate Ivan further. As soon as he did so, Ivan wrapped his hands around the boy's throat. The scene was very familiar from previous encounters, where Ivan would hold his arm around my neck and threaten me with my life. For a few more moments, Pravilov held his grip on the player's neck and then pushed him on the bed. With a maddened look, Ivan stood in front of us, motionless for about a minute, calling us names like *gnidi* (nits), *padli* (scoundrels), *suki* (bitches), *halyavshiki* (freeloaders), *pederasti* (pederasts), *evrei poganie* (smelly Jews), *fashisti* (fascists), etc. I thought my turn was next, as I was the main culprit of the situation, but it never came. Pravilov stared into the responding player's eyes and said he should have his own head on his shoulders and not listen to others. This turn of events I did not expect, but I was still suspicious that my turn awaited me sometime later. When this was over, he ordered all four of us to take out all the food we had in our bags. We laid the food out on our beds in front of our coach to see, and everyone was waiting for something terrible to happen. The anticipation was frightening, because Ivan looked like he would throw someone out the window from the fourth floor we stayed on. Nobody made a sound and no one wanted to move either. We stood there petrified. The room became quiet, but the silence was unbearable. *Not again*, the thought popped into my mind. The situation became so familiar that it was not a surprise to me anymore. I believed others in the room had the same feeling. *This would probably be another one of those "freaky" nights, when our coach spent it humiliating and abusing his players*, I wondered. I hoped it would be quick.

The next moment, Ivan backed away to have a better view of all of us and demanded that we eat all the food. "Because you only care about yourselves, you will devour all the food you have with you now!" he exclaimed. One of the players mentioned that he was not hungry, which we all found out soon enough was a wrong answer. Ivan dashed to him, throwing a hard blow into his stomach, repeating himself, "Zhri padlo (Devour the food, Scoundrel)." The punch had thrown the player a few paces back, almost knocking the nightstand behind him. The player began shoving in his mouth everything he had, and others followed suit. I particularly remember one boy taking a big bunch of grapes out, still attached to their stems. He finished the fruit and threw the stem in the garbage bin. Ivan noticed that and, in an instant, jumped to him. He hit his face with his fist with a full force. The delivery was hard enough to force the player down on the floor. The words "Zhri padlo vse (Devour all the food, Scoundrel)" sounded again. Ivan told him to take the stems out of the garbage and begin eating them. The boy began chewing on it, distorting his face in the process. For that he received another blow in the face and was instructed to eat fast and with a smile. Meanwhile, I and two other teammates finished our food and remained focused on the player with grape stems. He tried his best, but the bitter facial expression could not lie about the taste. It seemed to be inedible, to say the least. In approximately five minutes, the player made very small progress, so Ivan turned his attention at the others and asked us why we stood there without offering our help. No one responded, and each tried to avoid our coach's stare, afraid to draw his focus upon himself. We all stood with our heads down.

This time, Ivan turned the tables and made the other three players the villains of the situation. He told us that we reacted exactly like we would on the ice during our games. We only cared for our own hides, and what happened to others did not matter. As a result, he made it clear to us that if the grape stems were not finished in several minutes, we would begin punching each other in the face. All three of us moved in and took a piece of a stem. During my first bite, I realized the bitter taste would be tough to consume, but I was determined not to fail. I imagined that punching my teammate and receiving the same in return would not be a pretty scene. Disregarding the bitterness, I began chewing fast and, in a matter of few minutes, had all pieces in my possession swallowed. I noticed that everyone else was doing the same and completed their assignment quickly. When there were no stems left, Ivan growled, "I guess you do not want to punch each other in the face. That is okay, next time." He continued degrading and belittling us, using examples mentioned earlier and, eventually, walked out of the room, leaving us guessing if we should wait for his return or go to bed.

We stayed awake for a while and no one would mention a word from the recent event. I felt very bad for making a wrong assumption and letting others take the heat for it. Ivan did not lay his hands on me once during the whole episode, and never directly pointed his rage at me verbally. Knowing him well after many years together, I felt Ivan had reserved a "surprise" for me later. I could not remember any detail that passed his focus, and this was no exception. He never let a deed go unpunished. But not today, and I hoped not for a long time. I spent the rest of the evening and night not making a sound, feeling guilty in front of my teammates. I made them suffer the consequences. Perhaps, Ivan understood that hatred and contempt from the other players would be enough punishment for me, which would keep me feeling low and outcast. In any case, the anticipated punishment was never realized and a long time went by before I could feel more at ease.

Bus Trip (From Edmonton
to British Columbia)

In the winter of 1994–95, Druzhba-78 was on its second western Canadian tour. I was sixteen. The team traveled to Edmonton, Alberta, and British Columbia. We also visited Anaheim, California, and finished the tour by playing a series of games in the province of Quebec. During our visit to Edmonton, several incidents had happened that raised some questions about Ivan's purpose and methods. However, to my knowledge, those were not as notable as the trip we undertook from Edmonton to British Columbia. We were on the bus for many hours prior to reaching our next destination, and Ivan took advantage of this opportunity to literally test our loyalty and "love" for him.

After everyone was seated in their usual spots, Pravilov decided to move to the back of the bus. Positioned almost at the front, I could neither see nor hear what was happening in the back. I was simply leaning against the window ready to be called upon any second. After many years and numerous experiences dealing with my coach, I learned how to block my mind from any fearful or nauseating anticipation. I stared out the window, enjoying the scenery of the outside world. My mind was at rest, trying not to think of what could come ahead. I also noticed that our organizers sat in the front without any intention of looking back. They, like all previous organizers, superficially noticed the tension on the team and did not want to get involved. Who could blame them, when some players unexpectedly showed up with their cheeks the size of a watermelon and all Ivan would say was the boy had gotten into a fight with another teammate. They could see, but no one could prove anything. I heard some commotion in the back and turned around to look. Apparently, Ivan had been systematically calling one player at a time to the backseat for a long conversation. Each lasted for at least twenty minutes, but some did not return for almost an hour. Because my seat was located at the front, away from everyone else, I knew I would be one of the last and hoped the time would run out before we arrived at our destination. However, my hopes came to no avail and, eventually, my name was announced.

Walking down the middle aisle of the bus, I could not help but notice the gloomy and tearful faces of my teammates. No one looked at me. Everyone stared out their windows as I did just seconds ago. Their expressions were empty, like someone had put a spell on them. This was not an encouraging sight and my heart sank. My legs became heavy. My movement was slow, trying to delay each step and prolong my approach. As I moved through the aisle, the smoking smell had increased exponentially. Although our organizers and bus driver told Ivan not to smoke on board, he believed in his righteousness and deliberately ignored all precautions. The stench was unbearable, but that smoke was the least of my problems at the moment. As usual, I decided to adapt and go with the flow. My position would be neutral. Like before, I needed to leave my emotions behind and become a survivor. My focus was on what Ivan needed to hear and not what I truly believed in or thought about.

At last I reached his seat and noticed that he was lying on his back, stretching his legs across the aisle. I stopped there, facing the man I both feared and despised. For a few seconds he kept his eyes closed, ignoring my presence. When he opened them, the wicked smile appeared on his face. Ivan continued his silence and, with the bulging eyes that I had become accustomed to, stared at me, waiting for my next move. Like before, this maneuver was one of his mind games, trying to break the player at first sight. By forcing a player to begin the conversation, he seemed to be in triumph of winning the first battle. This was no different and the stare persisted until I broke the silence. I figured that making him begin would aggravate his ego and worsen my chances of getting out of this untouched. Therefore, I obliged and blurted out that I was there because my name had been called upon. I stood there petrified, looking the man in his eyes, the tactic I picked up long ago after noticing that he respected those who did so. His first response was a question. "What are we going to do?" he asked, referring to me by the nickname he had come up with a long time ago (he had a different nickname for each player, in addition to the general names mentioned earlier that he liked to call us on a daily basis). I continued standing there, quietly waiting for him to resume his inevitable questionnaire. I hoped he would say something instructional, but Pravilov lay across two seats, smiling and enjoying his moment. Now that I began first, he had a full superiority over me and had my mind at his will, or so he probably thought. He interlocked both of his hands behind his head and asked me if I loved him. Thinking of it as just another question that needed a satisfactory answer, I responded, "Yes." "Do you love me very much?" he followed with more vigor in his tone. I looked at him in disbelief. Now he sounded desperate for some affection, so I went along with it and answered "yes" again. For some reason, I began to feel that the situation had just taken another turn. Ivan never before asked me if I loved him very much. Needless to say, he was never just about himself in the conversation. He would always bring in my parents and my teammates. The mind games always included others to whom I had to measure my love and compare it with my affection to Ivan. This time, he was the only target of the conversation and I needed to be ready for a new trap.

The coach was not satisfied with the answer and persisted with another question. "Do you love me very, very much?" he asked, emphasizing the "very, very" words. I paused for few seconds before replying. The circumstances were new and I needed to reevaluate my position in the conversation. I always suspected that it could lead to a new trap and thought of my next response in greater detail. Answering "no" would mean I lied and a barrage of punches could follow. Answering "yes" would probably satisfy the coach, but my hesitation could draw some suspicion. I figured I hesitated anyway, so my answer was "yes." Ivan responded instantly by addressing my slow response, as I predicted. He hated my hesitation. I did so, since the day I joined the team, and Pravilov tried to "break" that habit using intimidation and violence. He never succeeded, but never gave up trying. This time was no different and I received a couple of blows on the jaw that forced me to answer quicker. So he repeated the question. Without hesitation, I answered "yes." "Good," he said, "you learn fast." Coming back to my slow response, he asked me why I hesitated. I told him of my pondering over my love for my parents and if I had a greater affection for them. He did not hesitate for any moment and asked, "And what have you decided?" My next response shocked even me. Unintentionally, my reply sounded like mocking of Ivan's intelligence at his inability of putting two and two together. I said, "I responded 'yes,' didn't I?" Without realizing, I caught myself taking great pleasure in the moment, cherishing my temporary triumph. The next instant, I saw Ivan's eyes peering out and his subsequent outburst coming at me louder and louder. He delivered another couple of punches and cursed me with all kinds of names like "*gnida*" (lice), "*padlo*" (scoundrel), "*evrey poganiy*" (smelly Jew)1}, etc.

The violent charade was over after a few more minutes of meaningless mind games that resolved to nothing. Ivan resumed his laying position, stretching his legs across the aisle. His next demand came as no surprise. "Prove your love to me," he announced. This question followed many of our conversations and, by now, I knew what to do. Unwillingly, I leaned forward and provided a hug. Although I resented the smoking smell and could not handle Ivan in any proximity, I understood the hug must be believable. So, I wrapped my hands around him tightly, taking no chances for any suspicion. He held me in this position for a minute or so and then asked if that was all the love I had for him. Ivan changed his tone to low and began stroking my hair. By now, I was simply relieved that my coach had calmed down and probably would not physically abuse my face any more. Previously, this change in tone and attitude meant I would be let go, but not this time. What came next became a shock that I could never recover from. After all the abuses and humiliations throughout my years on Druzhba-78, I thought I had experienced and seen everything that Ivan could offer. But no, there was more in his arsenal. He asked me to kiss him.

The request came so suddenly that I froze on the spot for a few seconds. I would neither move forward nor back and could not speak out for a lack of understanding of what it meant. All kinds of thoughts ran through my mind. Finally, I justified his request and kissed him on the cheek. For a moment, the idea sounded innocent, and it could probably be my only chance to get rid of him. But the coach would not let me go. His breathing became intolerable. Ivan's constant smoking became a burden for me to endure, and my face was inches away from his. For a second, my eyes became watery, probably battling the secondhand smoke. But Ivan took it differently and thought I was crying for him. Not a second went by before Ivan had my face in his arms. He pulled me in and said, "Kiss me on the lips." I hesitated for a while, resisting his grasp and thought that this was beyond my expectations and understanding. Now, Ivan really had gone mad. This time, he pushed the envelope too far. I asked him what he meant by kissing on the lips, to which he replied, "What part of kiss me on the lips you do not understand?" I looked at him in astonishment, not believing my ears and still trying to somehow deviate my focus from the reality. For a moment, I tried to think of a way to change the subject, but no solution could pop into my mind. Ivan's focus on the subject matter was too great. "Why do you stare at me like an idiot? Are you going to prove that you love me or not?" he impatiently began rattling, while simultaneously hitting me on the forehead with his knuckle like someone would knock on a door. I saw no other option to make this madness go away but to satisfy Ivan's wishes. I stopped resisting and let him pull me in. The experience was nauseating, to say the least. He told me to give him a French kiss, allowing my tongue into his mouth. My body tensed and without realizing it, I shortly began pulling away from Ivan's grasp. Pravilov held me in that position for about thirty seconds and then released the grip. I pulled away from his face, still sitting within his arms' reach.

Considering that I did not hold myself in the position for any longer than Ivan held me in his hands, I thought his mind games would resume. I expected an array of statements like "You do not love me" and questions such as "Why you were lying earlier?" But to my unexpected surprise, he only stared at me indifferently and ordered me to leave. He closed his eyes and ignored my presence. I had not moved right away. My instinct told me to stay put and see where the situation would lead. In my previous encounters, Ivan was known for yelling back that I was not permitted to depart, so I sat there quietly, waiting for the "order." In a few moments, he opened his eyes and pushed me aside, growling that I was no longer needed before him. "Call the next one," he declared. I slowly got up and walked back toward my seat. On the way back, I saw similar empty stares that had not left the other players' expressions. They continued looking out their window, making no attempt to glance anywhere else. I tapped on the shoulder of the next victim, reminding him of his turn and sat down in my seat. At that moment, I thought about my poor teammate and his inevitable fate. With no words exchanged, he slowly walked the same path I had just taken moments ago. Then I wiped my lips in disgust, not believing in what had just happened. From one perspective, I was relieved the encounter was not very abusive (by now, Ivan's intermittent outburst of his fists had become a custom and I believe many of us had gotten used to it), and a few punches on the face was not a big deal. From the other standpoint, my blood was boiling with rage and anger. He called us *"pederasts"* and *"golubie"* on many occasions, but this act demonstrated his own dubious behavior. From that point on, not only the rage and anger but also my suspicion had risen about his true self and orientation. *What a hypocrite*, I thought to myself about my coach. The incident had literally turned the tide of my emotional attachment toward Ivan. I could no longer handle his two-faced behavior and statements. Until then, I still felt part of a common cause despite all of the hard obstacles that Ivan provided, but no more. I saw the name of "Druzhba-78" and all that Ivan represented a complete lie. All the preaching he had done and all the "lessons" he performed made my stomach churn. I wanted no part in his undertakings in any foreseeable future.

Interestingly enough, this point of my life had marked the revival of my soul. No longer did I care about his beatings and humiliations. No more did I worry about making a mistake. His constant speeches and threats came into one ear and went out instantly from the other. I no longer felt burdened by fear. Coincidentally, my performance on the ice had improved drastically. I began eating better and working on my physical condition with greater enthusiasm. I felt a complete emotional detachment that transformed into a greater self-respect and understanding of what I wanted in life. I also began growing, reaching six feet and one inch from five feet and three inches in two years. An enormous weight had been lifted off my shoulders and all I had to do was to work hard toward my set goals. Nevertheless, the old habits would not go away and I continued to demonstrate my submissive patterns toward our coach. In my mind, there was no reason to aggravate the emotionally unstable individual who could, in any second, snap and end me right there and then. By surviving his wrath, I felt I would win my battle against tyranny. So, my silent fight went on until I felt the time was right to depart.

Western Canadian Tour, December 1994 - February 1995

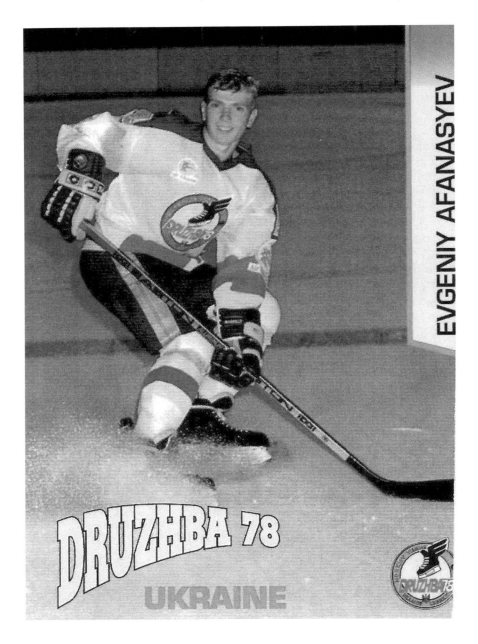

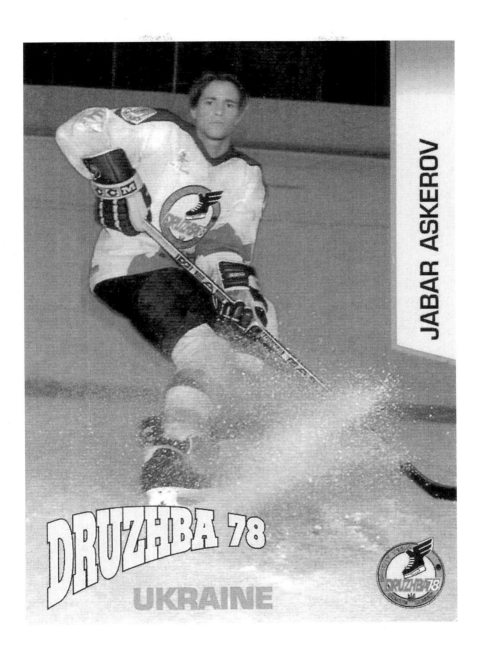

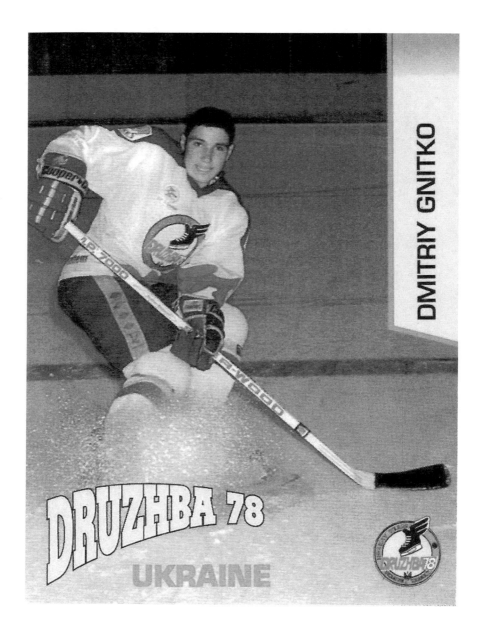

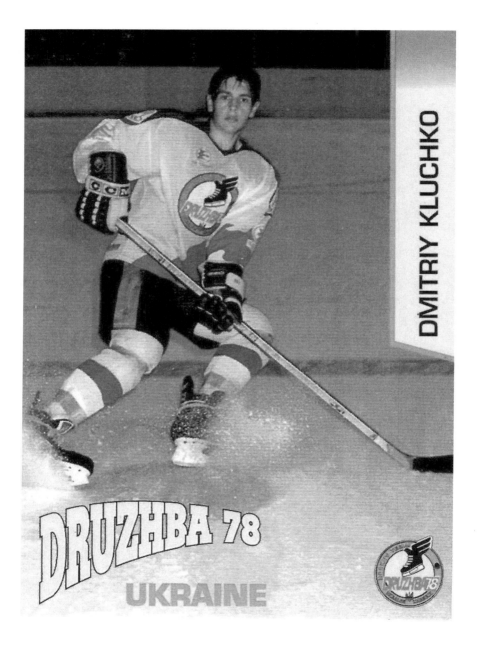

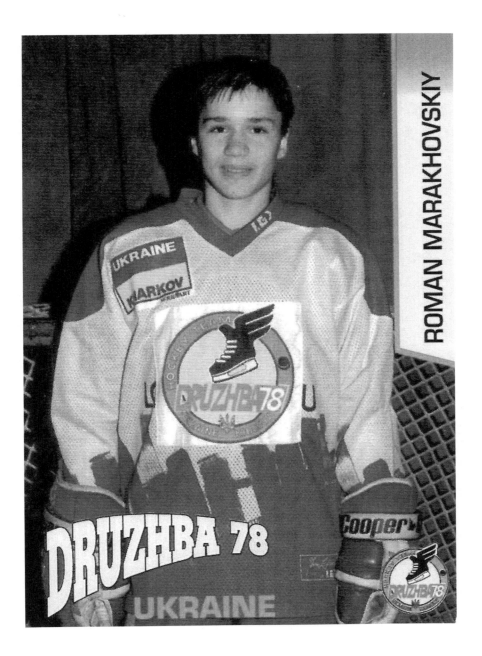

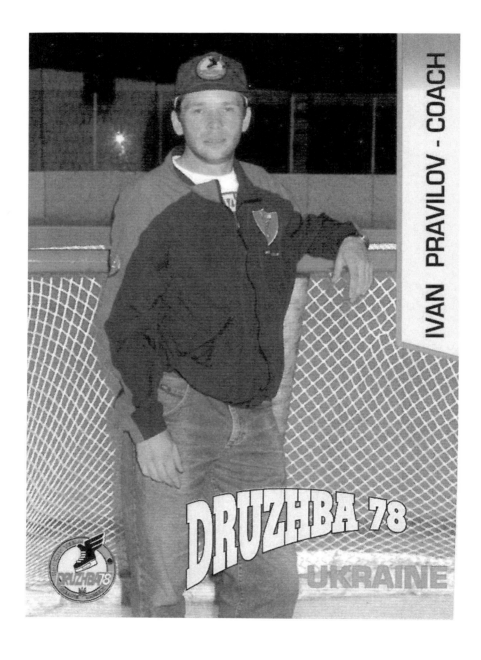

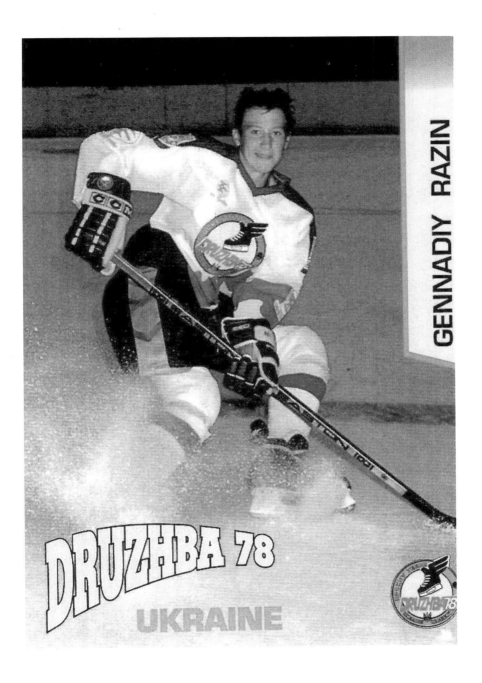

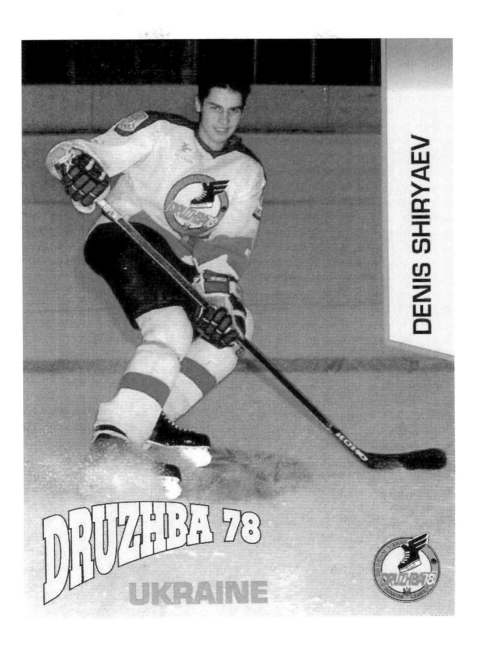

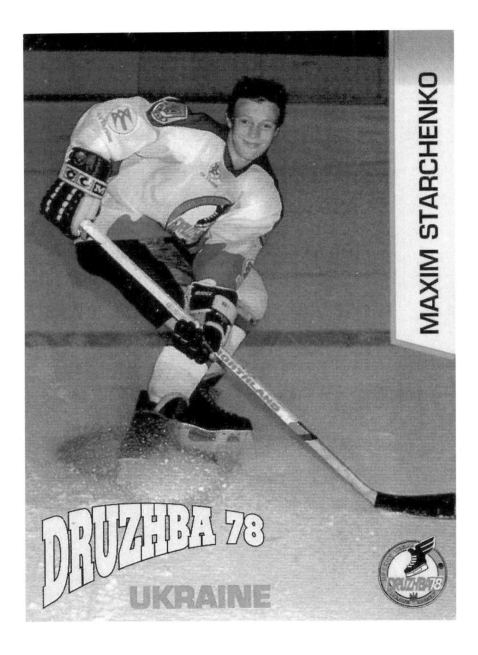

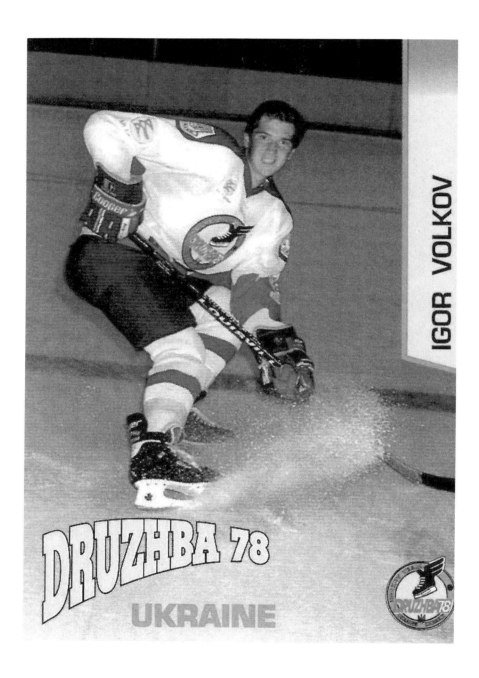

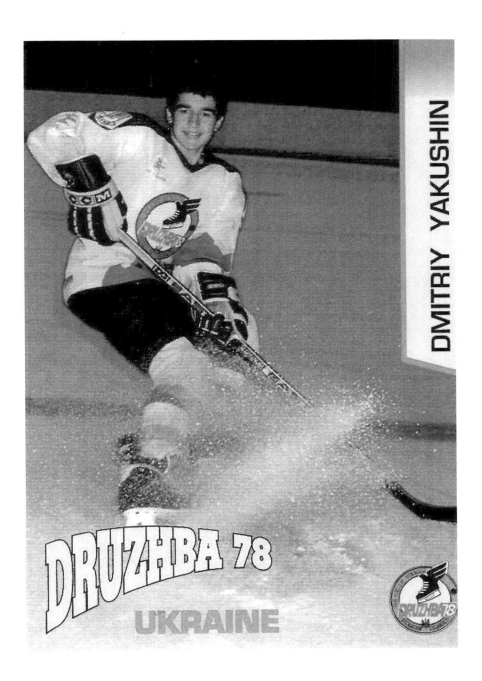

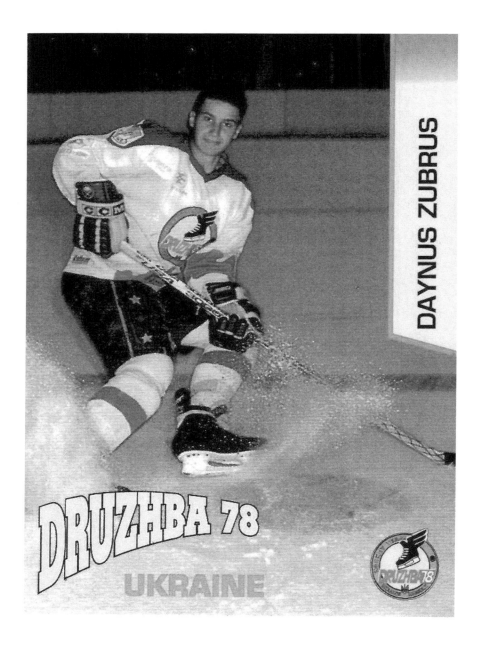

St. Leonard and Beauport, Quebec

The second western Canadian tour had almost come to an end, when the team was invited for another set of games in the east. We were to play a set of exhibition games and a couple of tournaments in the province of Quebec. Both tournaments provided incidents of their own, after which Ivan had to only save face and quickly leave for Ukraine with the rest of the team. The first set of games was played in St. Leonard, a small town not far from Montreal. The whole team stayed in a small hotel, which I believe was the critical mistake of the organizers. Not one soul on Druzhba-78 wanted to face Ivan on a regular basis, and placing us under the same roof was a recipe for inevitable disaster. At this point of our existence, Ivan's sanity was long gone. He began drinking heavily. He threatened each of us with all sorts of intimidating statements and violent outbursts. Living under the same roof also meant constant team meetings that Ivan loved to conduct so often. At any time during those meetings, he could unleash his wrath upon anyone and create another group scramble similar to the earlier experience in Detroit. At this point, no one on the team was safe.

By this time, the players were exhausted from the trip. We played around fifty games in two and a half months and no end was in sight. Everyone wanted to leave for home, but Ivan had other plans. He continued accepting invitations from teams and organizers without any regard for our health and physical condition. Half the team was hurt and could not compete, so we played each game with seven, eight, or nine players. Ivan also demanded a considerable sum for each game we played, a fact that I believe significantly affected our coach's decision to prolong the trip. He pushed us beyond any reasonable expectations and the competition kept getting tougher. We would always face select teams or some of the better hockey clubs in North America, so each game took a sizeable toll on us, physically and mentally. Eventually, our performance on the ice had deteriorated and we barely competed in each game. We tried, but there was nothing left in us. Physically, we could not push ourth so many players hurt. Mentally, I no longer cared about the results .mes and could not wait for the moment when we left for home. Ivan ly unleashed a barrage of his threats, and only by fear and punishment could he motivate us to go on. Behind our bench, during each game, he sounded like a mad tyrant who was losing control of his players. He understood that using physical force against us in public could endanger his "integrity" and reputation, so he would not let any outsider into our locker room during the intermissions and after games. That was his time to rule and make us suffer. Anyone in close proximity to him in the locker room could be his scapegoat. Each time we entered the room, he would lock the doors and let the fury soar. No one could flee this madness and, at some point, everyone received a piece of his "medicine."

The situation at the hotel did not help either. Very quickly, we noticed that it featured a pornographic channel, which, for our team, could only spell disaster. The disaster would not come from us watching it but from Ivan's interpretation of how bad it was for us. Ivan began blaming our hormones for bad performance on the ice and, during our team meetings, started to demand our "confessions" about the number of times we jerked off per day. Out of fear, or perhaps out of mere disregard for what would happen next, some players said twenty times, others mentioned thirty, and still others said they masturbated about fifty times a day. Our coach would laugh at the numbers, emphasizing how we could perform well after all this. He then took his insanity to the next level and decided that we needed to punish each other for our deeds. He would demand that we find a partner and start punching each other in the face. When someone did not provide a legitimate punch that satisfied Ivan's standards, our coach would approach and demonstrate how it must be delivered. I still remember my first punch on my teammate's face that barely brushed my fist upon his face. Pravilov noticed it and approached immediately. He delivered the punch with his all might and forced the player sitting opposite of me to fall down on the floor. When he got up, Ivan instructed him to show similar force on my face. Knowing he had no choice, the player delivered an excruciating blow that made me fall back and see stars flashing in front of me. Then our coach instructed me to return the favor, which I did. The hitting would continue for some time, and after about fifteen blows in each direction, we were ordered to stop.

During the tournament, Druzhba-78 lost two games. This was unheard of by anyone who followed our progress, and our coach continued to worsen his attitude toward us. The first game we lost was in the qualifying round, after which Ivan released his anguish and forced us to perform the punishment explained earlier upon each other. The insanity would not end there. When the team returned to the hotel, and after our post-game meal, we all gathered in one room for another session of delivering punches on each other. During this meeting, Ivan also demanded our confessions of the number of times we masturbated per day. When the meeting was over, I had a feeling the charade would not stop there. I was right; we still had a number of games to play, during each of which the players were forced to perform the punching "lessons" behind locked doors of the locker room.

When everyone dispersed to their assigned rooms, I rushed quickly to my bed and closed my eyes, lying there motionless. I made an attempt to block the entire meeting out of my mind and hoped to eventually fall asleep. But my tense body would not allow me to relax. I could not easily forget Ivan's sick form of entertainment and thought of upcoming brutalities. About twenty minutes had passed before my eyes became weary and I slowly began drifting away into a slumber. However, it was not to be. The next moment, Ivan entered the room. With heavy footsteps, he walked alongside of our beds toward the television. His usual hissing and munching noises added to the irritating heavy steps. He turned on the TV and put on the pornographic channel. Meanwhile, he smoked a cigarette and the smoke quickly filled the room. Pravilov sat down in the chair located in the corner of our room. A few minutes passed before he made another move. I could only imagine what was on his mind. Having naked people performing all kinds of sexual acts in front of his eyes, I hoped whatever he was plotting would not involve me. When he did move, it was toward our beds. At that instant, I held my breath. He stopped between our beds for several seconds, contemplating his next victim. I could feel the tension rising and thought that my slightly shivering body would give itself away.

Ivan leaned down, but not toward me. He lifted the cover sheet of my roommate lying across from me with orders to get up. My teammate pretended to be sleepy and moved somewhat unenthusiastically. He got up standing in front of our coach, probably puzzled and simultaneously frightened of whatever awaited him. Ivan sat down on the edge of the bed, making himself comfortable. He told his victim to describe what was happening on TV. My teammate could barely put two words together, obviously surprised at Pravilov's blunt request. He tried to explain, but only mumbles came out. As usual, our coach became irritated by this hesitance and raised his voice, asking for the same information. My teammate responded that a man and a woman had sex. That answer was not satisfactory for Ivan. "No, no, no, you tell me what exactly they are doing—be specific," he demanded. Thus the victim began a detailed explanation of the scenery in front of him. Ivan continued nagging him on and asked if the boy liked what he saw. After hearing a positive reply, my teammate was asked if he became aroused at what he saw on TV. The response was negative, and now Pravilov had my teammate at his disposal. Like previous mind games that the coach unleashed upon me, this was no different. His next question was, "How could you like what you see and not be aroused? Are you a faggot?" When the boy said he was not a faggot, Pravilov ordered him to prove it. I understood the player's position very well. Regardless, his responses would always lead to a losing outcome, and Ivan cherished such moments of feeling powerful and invincible. The player was probably stunned by this demand, thinking Ivan had gone mad (reminiscent of my thoughts and feelings during my earlier experiences with the tyrant). He was ordered to masturbate standing next to our coach and facing the television. "I cannot do it," my teammate said sadly. To which, Ivan responded, "Drochi Evrey (Jerk off, Jew)."

Meanwhile, the other two roommates and I were in our beds facing the opposite wall, pretending to be asleep. I held tight and tried not to breathe much. My movements were minimal, if any at all. In that position, I thought, Ivan had little chance of noticing my presence, making me a less likely next target. Although I felt that this could be similar to the Elektrenay test where everyone was included, my hope of evading this particular onslaught was still alive. Therefore, I laid there frozen, drawing as little attention to myself as possible. The boy began masturbating while Ivan encouraged him along. I repeatedly heard my teammate's plea that he could not finish. But Ivan kept at it and would not budge. "You will jerk off all night, if it takes that long," he declared repeatedly. The masturbation session continued for a long time. Eventually, it came to an end, although I cannot recall how it ended. I fell asleep before the conclusion and the next morning felt fortunate to having done so. I still do not know what ended up happening and never bothered to ask, as such instances were far too personal to discuss.

Eventually, the semifinal game had come. The team we played was one of the better hockey clubs in North America, and Pravilov probably foresaw the outcome before the game started. Considering we had less than ten players to compete with, our chances were not very good. Therefore, Ivan resorted to an array of threats in the locker room. He promised us the ultimate judgment night, where each one of us would stand in one room, jerking off while facing the other players. The game began badly for us; the opposing team scored twice in the first period. The scoreboard showed 1-2 against our team, and I was prepared for the worst in the locker room during the intermission. Ivan continued his threats, but held back on any physical abuse at that point. I suspected that our coach left the worst for after the game. As the game progressed, he would no longer point out our mistakes. The language I heard from him on the bench was profane and hostile. He would get in my face or talk into my ear from behind as I stood facing the game leaning on the board. His constant hissing sound and bulging eyes signified the impending onslaught upon the completion of this game. I tried to block his menacing expression out of my mind and focused on the game. At least, if we won, I thought, Ivan would leave his rage for the final game and we could live another day. However, the final score was 3-4 in favor of the other team, and now I, as well as everyone else on the team, was mentally preparing for what was promised to us.

We walked into the locker room with our heads down. Some players had tears in their eyes. I could not tell if this was because they were truly upset about the loss or frightened of what was to come back at the hotel. I was one of the first ones to enter the locker room. As I walked toward my seat in the back of the room, one of the players literally flew by me in the middle, pushing me aside. It seemed someone threw him across in anger and made sure the signal would indicate the magnitude of the situation. Apparently, Ivan could not wait for our return to the hotel and singled out one player to demonstrate his anguish. As the player flew by me, he lost his balance and fell on the floor. Ivan rushed toward him immediately, grabbing the player by his shoulders and pulling him up onto his skates. That was followed by another throw, only this time, the player connected with the wall next to me. The player lost his balance again and fell on the bench. Pravilov grabbed him again and dragged his body across the floor to the middle of the locker room. He commanded him to get up right away, but as soon as those words were spoken, our coach delivered a loud blow on the player's face. It sounded like something snapped, and I thought that Ivan probably broke my teammate's jaw. "Podnimaysa suka (Get up, Bitch)," our coach bellowed, with no remorse for his victim. When the player got up, Ivan delivered another blow that forced my teammate to fly across the room and hit the wall. The player landed a couple of feet from my seat, which forced me to react quickly. I moved aside to avoid drawing attention from the infuriated monster. *If this is only the beginning*, I thought to myself, *I cannot imagine what is coming at the hotel.*

The beating continued nonstop for about ten minutes, during which the player in focus had received excruciating blows and was called by many names and profanities. One blow would always be followed by another. My teammate flew across the room in different directions, trying to hold his balance and ground. On occasion, Ivan would not wait for him to get up. While the player was down, he stood above his body, holding him with one hand and punching him with the other. The scene made me shiver. This recalled my experience in Uzhgorod during the "soccer penalty kicks," and I never wanted to face that again. I felt the adrenaline pumping through my body with great speed. I kept my eyes down, focused on the floor, a technique I learned long ago to avoid Ivan's gaze and bring less notice upon myself. Periodically, I would raise my eyes to see that everyone else followed a similar pattern. No one dared to look up, hoping they would not be next on Ivan's list. While Ivan performed his violent "session," his victim tried to justify his earlier answers to Ivan's questions. I realized that our coach asked the player some questions in the hallway while the team was coming off the ice. The answers were not satisfactory, evidently, and my teammate fell victim to Ivan's rage and lunacy. So, the player intermittently made an attempt to answer between the beatings, but Pravilov would not allow him any time for it. He would repeatedly chastise the player for responding. There was no answer that could make his rage go away and all my teammate could do was take the onslaught and hope it would end sooner than later.

When the beating was over, Ivan told all of us that this was the example of what would come next. He told us not to expect any mercy and we would have to jerk each other off at the hotel. The name-calling and inevitable threats did not stop for another fifteen to twenty minutes. Then our coach suddenly stopped and walked out of the locker room. I took a quick glimpse at the other players and saw complete withdrawal. No one looked directly at each other, as everyone knew the meaning of what just happened. This time, Ivan elevated his "insanity" to a whole new level. How could I look in my teammates' eyes knowing the end result of our upcoming meeting at the hotel? For a second, I thought this could not be happening; perhaps, I would wake up in the morning from the nightmare described above, but to no avail. The very next second, the reality sobered me up quickly. I pinched myself to check my presence and felt a stinging bite. Each player changed his gear as fast as he could, as no one wanted to be the last one out. Such circumstances could put anyone in danger of Ivan's extra scrutiny, so I made a run for it. When I was out the door, my next step was to mentally prepare for the oncoming event. I could not allow myself to lose focus, because if I did, the suffering could be even worse. My strategy was to be ready for the worst, which meant Ivan could lose his mind completely and kill someone on the spot. The idea of jerking each other off equaled the thought of someone becoming Pravilov's dead victim. *How would I ever be able to talk to my teammates after such an incident?* I pondered. At that point, I was actually ready to accept numerous punches and beatings upon myself instead of experiencing such humiliation. Based on the dejected appearance of my teammates, no one had any doubts about Ivan's threats. In the past, when he spoke of a punishment, the topic would never be left alone. This time was no different.

When the team arrived at the hotel, everyone sat in their rooms waiting for what would happen next. We were instructed to go eat our post-game meal, which everyone accepted gratefully. "The longer we stretched the time, the more we lived," I figured. At the meal, no one said a word. Looking more like prisoners of war, we slowly ate our supper. Across the room, another team ate their meal. They smiled and talked, probably thinking we were a weird bunch. Their coach came to us, providing some words of consolation, but how wrong he was in thinking that our sadness was the result of our loss. Little did he know that he was actually making the situation worse because Ivan would undoubtedly use it against us. Our coach would flash his fake smile in return and, with a sarcastic tone, tell the other how badly we felt for our loss and that we were very upset. After exchanging a few more words, the other coach left for his table without any second thought of what was transpiring in front of his eyes. *Well*, I thought, *this is it, and no one would figure out what actually happened here*. Perhaps, the other coach had some suspicions about what he saw, but he would not believe that the seemingly genuine coach of Druzhba-78 could be a tyrannical sadist. Nevertheless, we all finished our meals and were further instructed to wait in our rooms until called upon. We could never have predicted the final outcome of this day.

Half an hour went by, then one hour had passed, and still no word for a gathering in a single room was announced. Of course, no one doubted the ultimate judgment would transpire, and as a result, each player was preparing for it. The time continued ticking and the anticipation became unbearable. Knowing my coach's past record of appearing in the room in the middle of the night, I decided to keep myself awake to be ready at any second. Several hours passed by, and still there was no sign of anything happening. Ivan seemed to have disappeared. Personally, I could care less what happened to him. The more he was away, the more we lived. I hoped he would not come, so we could go to sleep in peace without humiliating and embarrassing each other. When we were finally told to gather for a meeting, I braced myself, expecting anything, except what actually happened.

At first, Pravilov was not in the room. We all collected ourselves, making no sound and afraid to move an inch in the wrong direction. Ivan's calling card was always hiding in unexpected places to observe our behavior and catch us off guard. So everyone sat or stood still, positioning themselves as far as possible from the opposite corner of the room where the chair stood. We all expected Ivan to sit there, and no one desired to be in the forefront view. A few moments went by and our coach entered the room. I immediately noticed something was wrong, but I had no idea what an unexpected blessing it would be. Ivan looked perplexed and we seemed to be the least of his worries. He entered the room but did not walk toward his designated seat. "Stay here," he announced to us in a low tone and left the room as fast as he walked in. This was interesting because the only time Ivan spoke to us like a normal human being was either when we won a big game or competition or when important personnel came for a visit. I knew instantly someone important had come. I allowed myself some relief, understanding that it could probably save us from the promised punishment. Some players began to mumble, and soon, whispers about a missing player had reached all ears. I realized that one of us was missing in the room, and being so preoccupied with the oncoming event, I had not noticed his absence. This was just too much of a coincidence. The missing player was the one who had recently received the vicious beating from our coach in the locker room. I did not know what to think. From the moral perspective, I felt terrible for my teammate. From the survival perspective, I felt delighted that the madness might be stopped, at least for a while. The players who stayed with him in the same room told us that he was actually absent at the post-game dinner. I could not believe I never noticed it, but a similar reaction followed from many players who felt stunned and confused. *What does it mean?* the thought popped into my mind. The player was missing and no one knew where he was.

After about fifteen or twenty minutes of waiting, a police officer entered the room followed by Ivan. *This is new*, I thought. *No wonder Ivan had changed his approach and demeanor*. I tried to contemplate this new development of events. The officer asked all of us at once a few questions, including when was the last time we saw our teammate and if he said anything that could provide some clues toward his whereabouts. Then the officer told us not be afraid and, if needed personally, he was in the hallway nearby. *Wow*, I thought. I became astonished how Ivan was able to convince the officer about his innocence in the whole scenario. The coach's total personality had changed, because now he understood that his freedom hung in our hands. One word about the recent events and the ball would roll against him endlessly. He could not risk this fact and immediately changed his ways with us.

By now, the situation became obvious and we knew that our teammate had run away. The facts were still unknown, and the police had entered and exited our room several times without elaborating on any news. Later, we found out that the player left a note directed to Ivan. He wrote it during our dinner when he lagged behind in his room. The contents of it would not be disclosed until the police had left the building. Pravilov personally read it to us in a calm manner. The new development really shook our coach, and he seemed to be at a loss of what to do next. He told us that he spoke with the player's parents on the phone and explained the situation. *But*, I thought, *I wonder what version of the story you told them.* Anyway, he read the letter to us, which described all the "good" things Ivan did for the player in focus. He praised our coach for making him a better person and took all blame upon himself. *Great*, I could not stop thinking, *now Ivan would easily use that to defend himself.* And in my mind, he did. He also thanked Ivan for teaching him valuable "lessons" in life and apologized for not being able to make our coach feel about him any other way. The letter continued by apologizing to us (his teammates) for being a worthless and undeserving member of the team. The words were too coincidental, to say the least, considering that everyone was constantly reminded by our coach how worthless and undeserving of anything we were. Like the player from Doneck, who left the team earlier from Kharkiv, he explained his decision by saying that Ivan did not deserve the burden of his presence any more. He further mentioned he could not bear being a reason for the aforementioned sexual abuse Ivan had planned, and this outcome would better suit everyone involved.

I was amazed and disheartened by the letter. Although the player knew he would never see his coach again, he still wrote the letter from a positive perspective. The constant brainwashing and repetitive humiliation made the player really believe he was a worthless member of society and our coach was the savior who tried to remedy our bad ways. My teammate truly believed he deserved nothing in this world and could not justify his existence. I could not, at the moment, say anything more about myself either. No matter how positive I tried to be, the constant negativity provided no comfort for my soul. The letter proved that this player had similar feelings and his reaction might be a prologue of what awaited me in the near future. In any case, the brainwashing had helped Ivan not only control our fear but also manipulate our self-respect and self-concept. Because we were continuously "taught" to blame only ourselves in any situation, Ivan was able to protect his interests without much resistance. Knowing my own approach, keeping my parents in the dark about the atrocities Ivan committed, I had a feeling that the missing player's parents also did not know the whole truth. I actually felt that no parent knew the real extent to which Pravilov held his power over us.

Because the situation became so critical for our coach, I could exhale in relief. I knew that for some time, we would not be touched or humiliated.

Not one player in the room showed his emotions, but I am sure that all felt as if a big weight had fallen off their shoulders. The relief did not aid my conscience, however, as I really wanted Ivan to be caught and punished. Although we were saved, this was only a temporary solution. Soon, Ivan would be back to his own ways and fire at us with even greater force.

To say I was worried about my missing teammate would be an understatement. I knew he had no idea events would turn out this way when he woke up that morning. He had nowhere to go. He had left nearly all of his clothes behind, wearing only jeans and a T-shirt, and we were in the middle of a harsh Canadian winter. The circumstances could not be more familiar to me, as I had experienced a similar escape before. However, I could not compare the two because my attempt a few years prior had happened in my native city. I knew what to do and where to go. I had some kind of plan. This scenario was very different. Not only was the player scared that Ivan would pursue him, find him, and then punish him for embarrassing him in public, he also knew nothing about his surroundings. I believed that Ivan cared not for the player but for his own reputation and freedom. In a couple of days, our coach began blaming several people for hiding our teammate from him. He became delirious and soon started taking it out on us. But that came later. For the time being, I cherished the relief and hoped it would last longer. I felt thankful toward the missing player and truly thought he saved us from the embarrassment and humiliation all of us would otherwise witness and experience.

Shortly after St. Leonard, our team landed in Beauport, Quebec, for another tournament. This was one of our last stops, and everyone looked forward to the trip's end. We were glad that the organizers had placed us with local families; otherwise, I feared the result would be similar to what happened during the last competition. The only player who had to constantly remain with our coach was the translator. His fate was sealed as soon as Ivan decided to appoint him his "personal secretary." Anywhere Ivan went or lived, his translator followed along. The responsibility could not be any worse because by this time, Pravilov showed no mercy whatsoever. Anytime the player would appear with a bruise on his face or a swollen cheek, the rest of us knew where it came from. The outsiders saw it and some would casually inquire about the reasons. Not one player dared to respond telling the truth and Ivan would only smile and come up with another excuse.

The trip was near its conclusion, but the beatings did not stop. Playing with only eight or nine players against the top competition in North America did not help, and our performance on the ice continued to plummet. This was unacceptable by Ivan's standards, and he continued locking the door of our room during the intermissions and after the games in order to deliver the punishment. Personally, I began to anticipate it every time we played. Each time we saw him at the rink, the outcome would virtually always be the same. It had gotten to the point where Ivan stopped committing much of his emotions in the act and would simply sit in the corner and watch us punch each other on the face. "Ny chto druzhbani, vpered za raboty (So, my friends, get to work)," he would calmly say as soon as the doors were locked behind him. That meant to take our helmets and gloves off and begin exchanging the punches with neighboring partners. Ivan sat in one of the corners and repeated time after time, "Oh yes! That is how you must hit. That is how you must punish your enemy. You must not let your adversary outhit you." It would last until the *zamboni* (machine that resurfaces the ice) came off the ice and people in the hallway called us to come out. Only then did he instruct us to stop and put our gear back on. This was very simple to him now, almost a routine.

By now, we all knew what happened with the missing teammate in St. Leonard. Ivan started calling him and the locals who vouched for him traitors, also encouraging us to run if we had no desire to be on the team. He reminded me of my escape home from Anapa and said I should do the same now. I asked my coach where I would go, to which he responded by rolling and bulging his eyes out that it was not his problem. "I have fed you and clothed you to this point," he continued, "and now you can do whatever you wish." I think that the situation had reached such critical point that his constant violent threats could not reach our ears the way they used to. I believe he simply gave up and made no further major attempts to hold his powerful grip, at least for the remaining part of that trip. The intermittent remarks and occasional name-calling never disappeared though. Pravilov continued his typical behavior. Throughout the entire trip, for instance, Ivan never referred to me by my first and last name. He had a degrading nickname for each player and used it regularly instead of our real names. I was no exception.

Our team could not compete against quality opponents anymore. Ivan saw no other solution but to withdraw from the tournament before its completion. The organizers, of course, were stunned. But the players accepted the news with great joy. Each one of us wanted to leave for home and forget this misery. In a short while, we were on our way to Ukraine.

The next trip to North America in the coming summer of 1995 was our last one as a team. By now, Ivan already saw the inevitable consequence of players leaving the team to pursue their hockey careers and decided to make the best of it. We ran a series of hockey camps that provided our coach with needed resources for his next campaign to recruit a new generation of Druzhba players. The camps were very successful and he was able to make a significant amount of money, all of which went into the budget of "his" Druzhba organization. As Ivan probably predicted, a few players did stay behind in North America. Eventually, each one of them was called a traitor and Ivan continued to brainwash our minds that they were the lowest and worst individuals on this planet, although I believe our coach placed the rest of us into the same category.

To my knowledge, the players received none of the money mentioned above, except for casual $10 or $20 when our families could not provide for basic necessities like food. Since the first trip to Quebec, Canada, in February of 1992 and throughout the rest of the North American campaign that included eight separate visits for at least two months in duration, each player was to save every penny he received from various sources, including parents, fans, charities, communities, etc. Our coach collected the money at the end of each trip and recorded the amounts we handed in. The ones who provided the most were tapped on the shoulder and praised for their great contribution. One of the players, as I recall, had lost a $100 bill and reported the mishap. This did not sit well with our coach, and the player was blamed for pocketing the money for his own purposes. Ivan ridiculed and interrogated him in front of the team; perhaps, this was his tactic to intimidate the rest and send a message that such misfortunes would be considered a betrayal. I once made a miscalculation of the amount I held at one of the collection meetings. Instead of four $20 bills, I mistakenly calculated them as four $50 bills. So the $300 I turned in became $420 on Ivan's record. He gave me twenty-four hours to correct the mistake by finding the missing amount, which I had no idea how to retrieve. After asking him how I could do so when I had no extra money on me, his response was to figure it out on my own. "You can rob a bank for all I care," he said and rolled his eyes, accusing me of stealing. When the time had expired and I did not come up with the money, I was exposed to several ridicules and name-callings, not to mention punches in the face. It was my punishment for apparently pocketing the "team's" (read Ivan's) cash.

The New Generation

After the team's last trip to North America in the summer of 1995, Ivan began plans for the next generation of players. A few players had already left our team in North America and this had undermined our coach's plans to control our futures. He encouraged everyone to follow the "traitors" and mentioned that regardless of our decision, he would never change his ways. He understood that he no longer held us in his full grip and decided to use us to recruit a new group of potential hockey players before everyone had dispersed. Throughout the fall of 1995, we traveled all over Kharkiv running soccer tournaments similar to the ones that Ivan recruited me and others from. After about two and a half months, he had gathered a good number of future potentials and began the next chapter of his tyrannical reign.

When every player from my generation had gone to play in North America for different teams, only some kept in touch with the coach. Most of us, myself included, still retained a connection to him, albeit silent. I did not contact him for several months and tried to forget my nine devastating years with him. I enjoyed my time away, but I also felt sorry for the young players that Ivan said he would treat no differently from us. The memories of my first encounter with Ivan resembled the attitudes and naïve minds of the newcomers. Their parents heard a lot about Druzhba's accomplishments through local newspapers and television and thought their children would receive the best treatment and, possibly, a ticket into a better life. The children had a familiar spark in their eyes that I used to have during my first months on the team. They smiled a lot and believed their world could not have been a better place. When I realized that Ivan also included a number of girls in the group, I thought that this could only spell more disaster. I pondered over the situation and thought of the terrible punishments he would devise that included them. This would be a new level of his mind games and, perhaps, tortures. *If Ivan promised not to change his ways of treating his players*, I thought from time after time, *what could be in store for those children?* My heart was simply broken for them.

Upon my arrival back in Kharkiv in the spring of 1996, Ivan resumed his recruiting throughout the city, running soccer tournaments in every school. Because the city contained more than 170 schools, the task at hand was enormous. We assisted in finding players and establishing contacts. This continued until the end of the school year. Shortly after, Ivan asked me if I would want to be his assistant in training the next generation of players. The question did not surprise me. I was not the cream of the crop as a player in comparison to others, although several scouts had showed their interest during the past season. However, I understood his motive. He noticed my ability to relate well with children and this asset could really benefit his future expansion of the program. To this, I understood Ivan waited for a yes or no answer, because no gray area is satisfactory with our coach. Cautiously, I said I would want to help him with his endeavor, but in the back of my mind, the idea seemed suicidal. After this question, I began evaluating my possibilities. I wanted to continue playing hockey because this was the occupation I knew best. But I began to see Ivan's purpose for me sticking around. The circumstances did not fit well with my plans, and the more I thought about it, the more I felt trapped. Regardless of the turn of events, I continued my loyalty toward my coach and thought he would at least give me a chance to prove myself. Thus, I decided to devote that summer to my training for a new, upcoming hockey season and help Ivan with whatever he needed.

In the meantime, I noticed that behavior of many younger players who were recruited in the fall of the recent year had changed somewhat. They did not smile as much anymore and spoke fewer words, often sounding incoherent and foreign. They shied away from my questions, although I kept them to a minimum. Most stopped looking me straight in the eye. Their eyes were often fixed on the ground in front of them, and when they did lift them up, the focus would deviate to the side. The pattern repeated itself, as it did nine years before. I wanted to reach my hand to them and express my sympathies, but thought this could deter their relations with Ivan even further. My intervention would mean more punishment to them. Every passing day, I became witness to this depressing development, so I shifted my focus to the upcoming hockey season.

I thought I would end up playing somewhere, but the days went by and no prospect of a potential team had come up on the horizon. I was eighteen when the fall of 1996 had arrived. Ivan resumed his recruiting, and I began the routine of running soccer tournaments again. The three other players stuck around as well, and the four of us helped Ivan recruit the new set of young players. By now, Ivan would only show up briefly to find out if there were any potentials, then he would drive away to coach the earlier recruited players. The days became monotonous, but each time I showed up at the rink, the players behaved more like us a few years prior. Interestingly, we were kept out of the locker room when the meetings were conducted. Now, my other teammates and I were considered outsiders, and no outsider was allowed to be present. What was happening behind the closed doors or "iron curtain" only the players and Pravilov knew, but I had a feeling that it was not different from what had transpired during our meetings. The only question in my mind was if the coach had resorted to new mind games and physical punishments.

I did not have to wait long before discovering Ivan's abusive treatment. I am not certain to what degree his harassments had gotten to, but the fact of the children's fright could not be hidden. Before the summer's end, the players had transferred to a single school, #160, which was located only a few minutes' walking distance from the ice rink. At the end of each school day, they walked together to the rink and prepared for practice. Two of them always stayed behind to clean the classroom and, therefore, came a little late. Their arrival would often coincide with my appearance after my refereeing duties during soccer tournaments. So one day, when I entered the locker room, two of them sat motionless in the corner. Usually, upon my entrance, they were hurrying to get their hockey gear on to catch up with the others, but not today. The situation seemed strange, but the whole picture did not become clear until a few moments later. Both stared down on the floor and would not raise their heads to face me. I proceeded inside and casually said hi, hoping to receive a similar response in return. Not a second went by before the two players began weeping, continuing to gaze down at the floor. Tears slid down their faces. One of them could not restrain his hysteria and in no time started crying profusely. I saw him fighting the emotion but witnessed the depth of his dread for what was coming next.

Meanwhile, Ivan was on the ice with the rest of the team. No one else was in the locker room, and my initial thought was to provide both children some consolation. I froze on the spot and asked them, "What is wrong?" I thought this could help me figure out the reason for their behavior, but the question had the opposite effect. Their crying had increased intensely, and now I knew the circumstances were much worse than I originally assumed. They continued attentively staring at the floor. Both did not respond and repeatedly exchanged stares between each other to see if the other would volunteer. *Not a chance*, I immediately thought. The looks on their faces were very familiar, and I realized that Ivan had begun treating these children in a similar fashion to how he handled us in earlier years. I could not say anything. My words, I felt, would only aggravate the situation. I simply stood in front of them, thinking of ways to help ease their suffering. Over ten years I experienced Ivan's wrath and hoped there was a way to use it to help the children. Suddenly, an idea popped into my mind. Ivan never raised his hand and rarely spoke profanities and name-calling in front of outsiders. Because he considered me an outsider to this younger generation, I decided to sit in front of them when Ivan entered and prevent, at least temporarily, the oncoming abuse. Thus, I sat there quietly, waiting for Ivan's return.

Five to ten minutes had gone by before Ivan stepped in. His facial expression was furious. He stared at them with the bulging eyes he used to intimidate me with. Now I sat there, nonexistent, as no one paid any attention in my direction. The coach walked by me toward the already frightened players and began asking rhetorical questions that obviously needed no response. "Ny chto druzhbani, doigralis (So, my friends, have you played enough)?" one of the questions stated. Ivan's voice was exactly what I was accustomed to. It had the same hissing and threatening tone that Pravilov repeatedly used against his scared subjects. When the questions had been depleted, Pravilov turned his head in my direction, signifying this was not a place for me to be at the moment. I thought otherwise. This was my moment to stall him. I reported about my recent recruiting and contact information. I told Ivan about my conversation with the potential player. I hoped that by refocusing the subject of conversation, I could soothe some of the tension. However, his fury could see nothing else but the target at hand. Without hesitation, he "instructed" that I leave immediately. "Are you still here?" he asked me, growling at my face. I saw that I could not help the two players anymore and slowly gathered my things. Ivan could not wait for my departure and said to close the door behind me. As soon as I did so, I heard the lock turn from within the room. From this point on, my doubts about helping this tyrant expand his dictatorial reign over the children had waned completely. I saw no other option but to move on with my life separately, without facing further humiliation and abuse. This event stimulated my plans toward leaving Ivan and his tyrannical "empire" for good.

Last Days

The thought of finally leaving Ivan began preoccupying my mind around late August or early September of 1996. During this time, I helped him routinely referee soccer tournaments at numerous schools in the city. I got up early in the morning to travel to the schools Ivan had assigned to me in order to schedule new soccer tournaments. Upon the completion of the school day, I would visit other schools with previously set-up tournaments to referee and keep an eye on potential recruits. Ivan would arrive for a moment to ask if there were any prospects. If yes, he took out a video camera to tape them. He would ask me to record the players' contact information after or during the tournament. When there was not a player satisfactory to Ivan's standards, he departed shortly after without wasting any time. After a full day of arranging, scheduling, and running the tournaments, I was to arrive at the hockey arena for Ivan's further instructions in regards to the agenda of the following days. This similar pattern continued day after day during each week of the first two months of school, and with every passing day, I was more and more convinced that Ivan saw no other purpose for me but to be his assistant. From my perspective, being Ivan's helper meant to be his slave, doing whatever he willed whenever he wished. I would be reprimanded and ridiculed and constantly reminded how ungrateful and unworthy I was. With each passing moment, without any post-secondary education and no other life skills but hockey, I knew my existence would fade away without any remorse or gratitude from my coach. Ivan was the sole beneficiary of our labor and my entire existence depended on him. He was the only person with contact information for the other coaches and teams. At that point, I saw no hope in any future involving Ivan and, gradually, began planning my departure.

Could I ever be independent and self-reliant in such circumstances? The answer was no, and that fact scared me the most. Because Ivan controlled all hockey contacts, I could not make it out without his help. By the end of September, he stopped mentioning my future as a player and completely focused on my assistance, or whatever he had planned for me. When I asked him once about the prospect of us playing somewhere, his simple response was, "What do you worry about? Stay here with me to continue the legacy." After few additional moments, he added, "I thought this is what you wanted all along?" He looked into my eyes briefly and quickly turned away and left. This response shocked me deeply because I previously thought Ivan wanted me to prove to him I could reach something and become somebody. Apparently, the assumption was wrong, which forced me to reevaluate my priorities.

Sometime along the two months, around the end of September, one of the four players who stayed behind was thrown out. He was literally instructed not to approach the Druzhba locker room and was clearly told he was no longer a part of the group. Even though Pravilov had told all of us earlier that no one would ever be thrown out without their will, this player, for one reason or another, was no longer needed for his purposes. I could not believe what had happened. In the blink of an eye, our coach was able to throw his player on the street like garbage. The continuous preaching that lasted ten years about Pravilov's high morals had all been erased in that same moment. To that point, I thought, the least he could do was to help us initially and open some doors for all the years of our loyalty. But throwing someone out who had spent ten years helping building our coach's name and reputation proved Ivan's unworthiness of any degree of trust. Consequently, the player had nowhere to go and no one to ask for help, which really opened my eyes on what could happen to me later. Like me, he possessed no other particular life skills except hockey and, altogether, depended on Ivan's support. Ivan did not care what happened to him.

Because the left-out player was considered an outsider and now a traitor by our coach, I could not be seen with him at any moment. I was specifically instructed to keep him away from the locker room and, if he approached, to make certain his foot never crossed the threshold. My first reaction was shock. My next thought was why our coach would not allow this player back. For a few days the player was nowhere to be seen, but eventually, he began skating with a younger group. I kept my distance from him on the premises of the arena, so Ivan would not notice. But we would sometimes meet outside, where I found out that there was no actual reason for which our coach had banished him. Ivan told me to resent him, but I felt no different than before.

By now, the coach drank heavily, and his oblivious behavior and attitude could not be overlooked. Beer bottles could be found in many corners of his apartment. No one could cope with his temper. He began asking me and other teammates to sleep over one night at a time. I am not certain of the reason, but I believed he could not trust himself any longer to be alone. One of the four players (he originally came from Kiev) who stayed behind lived with Ivan in his apartment. When Ivan asked me to come over for a night to keep my teammate company, I witnessed something I had never expected my coach to do. I thought that over the ten years I had witnessed everything Ivan's fury had to offer, but again our coach had another surprise under his sleeve. Sitting quietly in the room watching television, I was stunned to see Ivan storming into the room looking back into the hallway and holding what appeared to be a Xerox machine in both hands. He turned his body completely facing the hallway and began screaming profanities on the top of his lungs. On the other end of the hallway stood his sister, who listened to this nonsense in full disbelief. The barrage of curses came at her so fast that she could not even respond. Ivan's face turned bright red, and I believed nothing could stop him now. All I thought about at this moment was how I would sleep through the night without becoming a victim. Anyway, profanities were not sufficient to cover Ivan's rage, and the next thing I heard shocked my ears even further. "I have all these boys who are willing to die for me, and they will cut everyone's eyes out if told to do so," came his aggressive verbal attack. *He is mad*, I thought. This man never ceased to surprise me and continued still. His rage reached new limits, and now he was taking it out on his sister. *First of all, I do not know if I would ever be able to do so, and second of all, not for you*, I pondered shortly after. Then another thought came to my mind, *This man is a lunatic. How could anyone argue with him about anything when he threatens his own sister with such things?* After all the years of tyranny and abuse, he actually believed in his invincibility behind our backs. He continued his pose holding the Xerox machine in both hands and threatened to throw it across the hallway. In one instant, he swung his arms and, with full might, made it happen. Only the machine was too heavy. It ended up landing not far from his feet, shattering in pieces. My teammate and I sat in the room motionless and speechless. All we did was look at each other and, without further dialog, decided to turn away toward the TV. The door behind us closed, and Ivan did not appear for a while. Shortly after, we decided to retire for the night. The next day, I discovered that my teammate slept fully covered by his blanket for the purpose of not drawing any attention from the coach upon his arrival. I did the same. *What a night*, I thought, *and this is the kind of future that awaits me*.

With time, my thoughts of leaving Pravilov grew in strength. I was contemplating on how I could approach him and where my departure would lead me. All these variables created an obstacle to my decision. I knew that as soon as Ivan considered me a traitor, all hockey doors would be closed and joining the army would be my only option. I also considered the willpower of facing my coach and thought that I might not be strong enough. After all, Pravilov managed to persuade me to return before, and he could do it again. Such a scenario was not an option. The third concern was my parents, who did not fully support me on the issue. They instructed me to wait longer for the events to develop, and perhaps my coach would help me later. I understood this was hopeless and explaining myself would not help the situation. I also realized the enormous magnitude of my decision. I felt helpless. The power was not in my hands. All the odds seemed to be against me, and I questioned my own survival afterward. However, my awareness of Ivan's control over my life had encouraged me to make my decision fast. I recognized that for the past ten years, I was not allowed to think for myself and build self-esteem. I was not considered an individual, but a number in the group. I knew nothing about myself and could not survive without the person who would never give me any credit and encouragement to go on. I was ready to live on the street, but this would be my own life instead of constant misery and regret in chains. If I died hungry and cold, I would be free in doing so. Thus, for the first time in my life, I decided to face the demon directly and walk away with some dignity. This was it, and without discussing with my parents my immediate intentions, I followed my gut, changing my life forever.

On one of the weekend evenings during the first week of November in 1996, I left my house with one purpose in mind. Without notifying my parents, my decision was made that tonight, I would return a free man. What the future held for me was not important at this moment. My entire focus was on facing my coach. This was a historical event in my life. I was preparing myself for the confrontation, but to make sure Ivan would not do anything stupid and violent, our meeting would happen in public. Understanding that this episode could take a long time, I still hoped for a chance of quickly ending the moment. Preparing for this instant for a long time, I saw no way back. My mind was settled on the present, but was I really ready to take on the next step? Who would I call? Who would I ask for help? Was there any prospect of post-secondary education? Would I be unwanted in my parents' home, when my father reminded me on many occasions of his early leave from his parents to provide for himself? All these questions still bothered my mind, but in order to go on, I needed to direct my complete focus at the present. Any doubt could easily redirect my decision, so I blocked the future uncertainties and continued on.

I stepped out of the bus #11 and now had another ten minutes of walking to reach the hockey arena. They were the fastest minutes of my life. My legs felt heavy and shaky. I delayed the moment a bit longer by shortening the steps and enjoyed the cold wind on my face. I could not know what waited for me next. Expecting the worst reaction from my coach would be the easiest way to deal with any response. I tried to calm myself down, but the heavy feeling persisted despite all of my efforts. Different scenarios had rolled through my mind, each consecutive one worse than any that came before. Now, the arena drew closer. I kept my mind focused on planning my introduction and presentation; otherwise, I could change my mind in a heartbeat. Apparently, this was harder than I originally thought it would be. I fought myself every step of the way.

My plan was not to get caught in an isolated area. After experiencing Ivan's recent outbursts and demeanor toward the new generation of Druzhba players, I needed to walk away quickly. I wanted to experience the freedom of my mind and my soul before anything happened. I wanted to see the world with different eyes, regardless of how terrifying it was. I wanted to eventually prove myself worthy, but on my terms instead of Ivan's. With this plan in mind, my feet carried me over the arena's threshold. Feeling like lead, they took me through the enormous hallway to the exit door from the ice rink. There, I decided to stop and wait. Ivan would sooner or later walk by, at which moment I would seize his attention and make the best of the situation. A few minutes went by. The younger players walked through, sounding their greeting in my direction. Other people passed me back and forth, not paying attention and minding their own business. After about five additional minutes, my coach stepped through the door from the ice. He looked the other way, giving some instructions to the younger players. Then the coach turned his face and continued in my direction. I thought he would stop, but his focus was on something else that made him walk through like my presence bothered him the least. This was my moment. I needed to act upon my plan instantly before my mind was changed. I said, "Ivan Nikolaevich." This was enough to redirect his concentration. He stopped and asked, "Chto ti hochesh (What do you want)?"

I immediately told him we needed to talk. I was surprised at the shaky tone of my voice and my face probably looked red from anxiety. My body felt petrified and my coach quickly realized that something important would come out of my mouth. He took on a serious stance, waiting for my next words. I looked him straight in the eyes and said this was my time to leave the team and him. Expecting an onslaught, I was prepared for anything, as long as he would let me go eventually. Instead, he reflected a smirk and, with a smile on his face, responded that I was not on the team and not with him for a long time. "Do you really believe you were a part of the team?" he uttered in reply. "This is my team. It was never yours or anyone else's. Now you can follow all the traitors. You always were ungrateful for everything I did for you, and this proves that your life was a lie all along." I listened to him carefully, taking in every word. Holding my ground, I would not move anywhere to the side, as this could mean a suicide. I could feel Ivan beginning to fume. He fought his ground, trying to demonstrate his composure, but the constant change in his facial expression and slight moaning presented the opposite. I needed to be firm to survive this and make sure he did not drag me into an isolated area. So I kept standing there without moving a limb. Shockingly, he did not cover me with the profanities he used to before. Once in a while, words like fascist, traitor, ungrateful, Jew, worthless, etc., left his mouth, but I believe he was more focused on the idea that I actually decided to leave him. I could not but notice that the event took him by surprise, and throughout the first half of our conversation, he could not seem to find an explanation for my resolution.

This realization gave me more strength, knowing that my coach was not invincible after all. I felt an upper hand for the first time in ten years with him, and hoped the moment would last until the completion of our dialog. I cherished it. Understanding that sooner or later, Ivan would find a way to turn the table around, I simply blocked his responses and waited for an end. I began feeling calm and self-assured. For some reason, his questions and responses could not penetrate my mind. This was, indeed, a great feeling. Nevertheless, Pravilov continued to search for answers and asked me about my next steps. I hesitated to answer. I could not reply because I had no real plan. Whatever came out of my mouth was not clear and now, impatiently, Ivan demanded, "Have you bit your tongue?" I said, "No." But as soon as the word was uttered, I sensed familiar fright in my voice. I could not believe how quickly the table has now turned, and Ivan was on the attack. He persisted, stepping forward in front of me. This made me nervous and now I fought for my balance. *This is not happening*, I thought to myself. *I should be stronger than this.* My feet stood still and the rest of my body would not move an inch. I tried to make the best of the situation, but Ivan knew me too well and would not back away. "So what is your plan?" he asked me again by elevating his voice. The first thing that came to my mind was Canadian contacts. Thus, I told him that I would probably make an attempt through them. He smiled again and said, "Call them and run to them, but they will not save you." He also added he knew all along of my intentions and waited for how long this would take. Then he asked me, "What if they do not help?" This time, my response was simple, that I would join the army. He did not provide further comments, staring into my eyes with a grin on his face. The response apparently pleased him.

The next second, his grin disappeared and I was told to leave. "Poshel von, gnida (Get out, lice)," he said in the hissing voice that I was so accustomed to. Not believing my ears, I continued standing there waiting for some kind of trick on his part. It never came and the words were repeated again. Not understanding why he let me go so easily, I slowly turned around and began strolling away. I expected something to fly in my direction and hit me on the back, perhaps a knife or something heavy. But with each consecutive step nothing happened. I could not fathom what had just transpired. The entire conversation lasted about ten minutes, and I was on my way out unscathed. Never had I expected this to happen so fast without any consequences, so my next thought was not to trust the madman.

On the way home, I felt elated but also suspicious. Several times I tried to quit in the past ten years, but he continued to pursue me. He would not let it rest. I also thought about why he would let me go with such ease. This was different from before, where my attempts to leave were very hard to realize. The two contrasting scenarios had boggled my mind, and to be on the safe side, I decided to stay home for a while and not be seen anywhere on the street. As a result of my suspicions, I spent the next five days at home, making no contacts with the outside world. As expected, my parents gave me no support in my decision but at least said that what happened was in the past; nothing could be changed and now we needed to think of alternatives. My dad reminded me of the army option, whereas my mother was persistent in continuing playing hockey. Personally, I enjoyed my first days of real freedom and cared less about my future. This was the moment I wanted regardless of anyone's remarks. Then after five days in "hiding," my former teammate who was thrown out for no reason came for a visit. He asked me why he had not seen me for the past week, to which I explained the whole situation. He smiled and told me to continue skating with him with another younger team. He did not need to persuade me much, and within the next few days, I was back on the ice.

The New Life and Road to Recovery

The first day I showed up at the ice rink, I could not relax my nerves. After my sudden departure from Druzhba-78 and final conversation with Ivan, I constantly expected my former coach to jump out of any corner and shower me with numerous punches and kicks. I avoided isolated areas, trying to keep myself safe. I spoke with one of the coaches from the younger team and was allowed to skate every day they practiced. I had no hockey gear, as every piece of equipment I had was now in Ivan's hands. I gathered some scraps of old worn and torn equipment. Other coaches readily supplied me with it and said I had nothing to worry about. The day went on and Ivan appeared several times within the premises of the ice arena. A couple of times, he walked by and purposefully gazed in different directions. This was a sign I no longer existed in his realm and my presence to him had a similar effect as any other stranger. I still believed he hated me for the "betrayal," but the fact that he seemed to be ignoring me actually helped to ease my tension. My mind would never rest completely for some time, remembering the unpredictable nature of Ivan's violent outbursts, but I slowly began to believe he truly cut me out of his mind for good. Unlike in the past, he would leave me alone and let me be. After I finished my first practice outside the reigns of my sadistic former coach, I felt a little joy. On the way home, my former Druzhba-78 teammate asked me if I was relieved that nothing terrible happened that day, to which I replied that I could not figure it out. I knew I was cautious and apprehensive at first, but with time, the initial tension had faded away. So, I responded about my joyous feeling that no more humiliation and abuse from him awaited us in the future. For the rest of the way home, both of us discussed the steps we would take to accomplish our alternative plans. But none of us touched on the subject of Ivan and his endeavors. I was glad to leave the topic alone for the time being. I wanted nothing to spoil my present cheerful mood.

With each consecutive day, I gained confidence in Ivan's indifference toward my presence and was able to rationalize my next move. In theory, I faced two options. The first one led me to the army, where no promising future awaited me. The second one was to continue skating in case something came up. My father encouraged me toward joining the military. My mother, on the other hand, insisted that I pursue hockey. In reality, I saw no other choice but the army. Half the hockey season had gone by at this point, and I had no idea how I would be able to find a team, since Ivan controlled all of my former contacts. I declared my decision to my parents, to which my mother protested and yelled at my dad for encouraging otherwise. She became hysterical and began crying and pleading that I ask some of my North American hockey contacts for help. The next day, my mother and I had a profound conversation about the prospects of my and the rest of the Starchenko family's future. My two younger sisters, she explained, were looking up to me, and my failure would be a tremendous blow to them. If I gave up, they would probably do the same. "You must go on," she cried to me, holding my hands as if this was our last dialog. "We have no resources to help you with anything, and you should give yourself a chance into a better world." She repeatedly mentioned that if I chose the other option, I would probably live in the same ragged conditions as we always did. She was persistent and would not give in to my pleas that I probably should simply join the army. She was adamant that I stayed my course and constantly encouraged me to move forward.

Her outcry touched me deeply. After many unsupportive decisions throughout the past ten years that I experienced from my parents, my feelings toward her had gotten warmer and warmer. Her openness gradually gained much of my trust and I felt she was finally becoming my friend. Consequently, I decided to continue skating and contacted several friends from North America for further assistance. Although only a few reliable contacts existed, my mother hoped I could catch a break through one of them. As a result, I did not stop training and skating in the hope that something would come of it.

My first break came not from my contacts in Canada and the U.S., but from our own town. One of the Kharkiv coaches was offered a coaching position in the Russian league for Perm "Molot." He offered to let me come along. Another former Druzhba teammate was also invited and both of us took on this journey to the Ural Mountains in Siberia. There, I enriched my professional experience, but after few months, the time came to leave for home. Upon my arrival, another coach propositioned an option of going to Canada to play tier two junior A hockey, although there was also a lucrative offer in the Russian league. I was not drafted in North America; thus, I had to settle for tier two and move up the ranks afterward. There was no other way around it. I also understood that playing second tier could open the doors toward a full athletic scholarship in an American university, and if such an opportunity presented itself, I would be foolish to pass it by. So, the decision was made to pursue the hockey route in North America. But the journey to get there would not be so easy.

The junior team in Canada that invited me to play for them had arranged for plane tickets in early August, but before my departure, one last step was needed. I travelled to Ukraine's capital city of Kiev in an attempt to obtain a Canadian visa and, when my turn came, the clerk explained that the room in my passport for visas had run out and a new passport must be presented. After I questioned her about the possibility of a temporary document that would allow me to travel, among other inquiries, all pleas came to no avail. The news was devastating.

Because I had reached the age of eighteen, all paperwork must be processed through the army, including the application for a new passport. I knew there was no way the military would let me get away with this and now I was at an impasse. My heart sank. I left the Canadian embassy in total shock and needed to sit down. Even my mother's earlier encouraging words could not help. I found a nearby bench and sat there motionless for almost thirty minutes, with my mind running two hundred miles per hour. I thought of different possibilities, but each one of them came to only two possible conclusions. First, I needed to find a personal contact who would pass the paperwork through proper channels. Second, because the Ukrainian economy mainly functioned in the black market, I required cash to pay everyone off. How much? I did not know, but my gut told me lots of it.

I called my parents shortly after and was told to get home. "We will talk about it in detail at home," my father said to me. Upon my arrival, I phoned the coach who set up my contact with the Canadian junior team, explaining the scenario. The conversation with him ended terribly for my sake. He told me I made him look bad and now I was about to lose the opportunity. My only solution was to promise I would remedy the situation right away and complete all necessary steps to redeem myself. Although he understood what was involved in the process, I was given a limited time window within which the hockey team in Canada would still await my arrival.

My next move involved a short conversation with my parents. Again, there was a conflict of interests between them. My dad continued supporting the military route, whereas my mom pushed for the hockey road. This ended with another emotional outburst, but my mother would simply not give in. She burst into tears and began another lecture of how miserable our living conditions were, which would not be an option for her children if the chance still existed for something better. This resilience on her behalf encouraged me to continue my original path and make the best of it while the opportunity has not been lost yet. The next day, I called several parents of the former Druzhba teammates, asking them for any personal contacts they had in the army registration offices. To my luck, one of them had already gone through a similar process and was able to provide me with the phone number of someone who could help me. We set up a face-to-face meeting, where I discovered that the process would cost me $900 in cash and it would take about four weeks to complete. I almost froze on the spot because the amount seemed unattainable by Ukrainian standards, and if not for my mother who sat right next to me, I would probably lose this arrangement. She noticed my petrified facial expression and, without knowing if the money would ever be in our hands in time, responded that I would deliver within the designated time frame. One of the conditions we were given was that the amount must be paid in full before the process began. Although I suspected a scam, the parents of my former Druzhba teammate told me the contact was reliable. We tried to negotiate breaking the payment in two parts, one before and the next one after the services were provided, but the guy would not budge. Apparently, I was just another person to him who attempted this scheme and he could easily dismiss my case, or so he claimed. Understanding that the power was in his hands, we agreed to pay in full as requested.

After establishing the contact, the money became an issue. I had some savings from the few months I spent in the Russian league, but needed much of it for phone calls to North America and other expenses. Therefore, my next step involved calling everyone in Canada and the U.S., whose phone numbers I possessed, asking for their help. Deep down, I believed the money I spent for the phone calls was wasted and no assistance would come of it, but the picture of my mother's tearing eyes and her adamant attitude elevated my spirits to continue. My mother told me she prayed for me every day and knew that God would send someone to my salvation. I did not believe her, but eventually, one of the calls was answered. One of my former boarding hosts in Edmonton, Canada, extended his hand and sent me the amount needed for the process. This time, I was able to contact the Canadian junior team personally with good news, but being afraid of the time limit for their patience, I lied about the length that the process would take me to complete. As soon as I received the promised amount, I delivered the money to our contact and set the process in action.

Very soon, I found out that my file did not exist in the records. Although I went through much of the process at fifteen years of age, where representatives came to our school for physicals and other information, my file, apparently, was lost somewhere along the way. To say I was surprised would be an understatement because I never thought that such records could be ever overlooked by the government officials. It meant the process now needed to be done from scratch and every step must be performed just like three years before. I feared this would significantly lengthen the process and decrease my chances of getting to Canada in time. Meanwhile, I continued to mislead my Canadian contacts in order to keep this opportunity alive.

One of the steps involved a physical examination. I was afraid that the supervising doctors would not allow me to pursue my agenda and would, instead, consider me well fit for my military duties. Because there was nothing physically wrong with me, other options must be considered. Well, I remembered that about three years prior, I had damaged my back during one of the hockey practices. I visited one of the hospitals afterward and, for one reason or another, received a note that my seventh vertebrae had been fractured. Back then, I understood that the fracture would mean I could not walk, but my abilities to do so were just as good as any other person next to me. I continued practicing, but kept a copy of the record just in case. Now, I needed those records more than ever. I immediately used them to fix my problem. I notified my contact about the situation, so whoever he instructed about my case could pass the records along. It took some time, but the information helped significantly. It was explained to me that without it, I would have had to come up with extra cash to grease someone on the inside. I guess I caught my luck for once and thanked the incompetence of the prior doctors diagnosing my back problem three years ago. Accordingly, my file now stated I could move along with the process.

Eventually, after two months of patiently waiting for the results of every step, my contact arranged a final meeting where I would receive the official allowance to temporarily forgo the army. Again, my mom traveled there with me in case I stumbled like during our first arrangement. We arrived there at nine in the morning, but the contact did not come out until ten o'clock. He told us that he needed a final signature and a stamp from the colonel inside his building. We just nodded in confirmation and continued waiting in the hallway. Another couple of hours passed before he appeared before us. The news was not good. "I have a hard time catching the colonel, so if you want, you could go home and come another day," he told us. This really aggravated us, but through squeezed teeth and a distorted smile, we sat there without moving anywhere. By now, the time was one o'clock and my mother and I quietly discussed the last encounter. We determined that our contact was trying to extort additional payment, but because the deal was already arranged, we stood our ground. At about four o'clock, the contact appeared again with bad news. We stood in front of him motionless, asking when we should come again. His response was that we needed not to show up another time because he had completed his part of the bargain. Not comprehending what that meant, we exchanged puzzled glances. *Now*, I pondered, *he really pushed too far*. The next second, with a big grin on his face, he pulled the document out with a signature and a stamp that allowed me to leave the country temporarily. At that very moment, I did not know how to react. I wanted to punch him in the face for his untimely humor, but my instincts prevented my violent reaction. *Let him enjoy his moment of empowerment*, I thought to myself. *He is not worth the raucous*. We thanked him for his services and wished him the best. Later, my mom confessed that she wanted to strangle him, to which I responded that my thoughts were no different. However, we had no time to spend our emotions on such details. After all, we had the document in our hands and it was now time to focus on the next step. I immediately notified the Canadian hockey team about the good news and told them I had only one more step to get the passport.

The following day, I gathered all necessary paperwork toward my application for the new visa passport. Because the process ran through Kharkiv militia headquarters, I caught another break. Initially, I thought I would have to come up with another chunk of cash to pay someone off. However, one of my good friends was a media correspondent and, through him, I was able to pay only what was officially required (about $20). He knew a highly respected official in the headquarters office. After contacting the official, he soon let me know that everything was set. I could apply for the passport. Shortly after, I submitted the papers and paid the aforementioned sum. The contact also helped me to speed up the process and, instead of four weeks, I received my visa passport in two. When I saw it in my hands, I could not believe that my first name was misspelled, where Maxim was changed to Maksym. Were they really that illiterate and could not read my application? But at this point, I cared less about the name and hoped my contacts in Canada had not given up on me. When this happened, the Canadian team rescheduled the tickets and now I was on my way to the Canadian Embassy in Kiev for a visa. This time, there was no problem. I got the visa and was ready for departure on November 1, 1997.

What an experience, I thought to myself. After all the turmoil and uncertainties, I was finally ready to leave. I guess my mother's prayers had been answered. But by the time I left Moscow on the plane to Montreal, Canada, I had no money left. Everything I had saved from the past hockey season in Russia, my Canadian friend's contribution of $900, and some input from my parents had been spent dry. I had only $34 in my pocket and was happy to have it. The cash was one of the last resources my parents had, but they were willing to send me away with something, instead of empty-handed. *I will never forget their sacrifice*, I thought, and hoped that some time I would be able to pay them back. On the day of my departure, my parents bid me farewell and instructed that if a situation presented itself to get an education, I should not hesitate. Soon, I was on my way to Moscow and, eventually, to North America. Only once, since then, have I returned home to see my family and friends.

Upon my arrival in Joliette, located between Montreal and Quebec City, I was greeted well. Because I had no hockey gear and had not skated for the past seven months, I requested some time for acclimatization and some new gear. Both were granted. After a few days, I began skating with the team and began a new chapter in my hockey career. I played well and after one of the games, Brown University's assistant coach came up to me, asking all the appropriate questions. He told me that if I took and passed the SAT exam, they would happily offer me a full ride athletic scholarship. That, of course, elevated my spirits, but I needed advice about the proposition. The next day, I called Bob Bruce in Edmonton and explained what had happened. I also asked him about my chances of passing the test, because I barely knew conversational English, and I definitely knew nothing about formal English. He expressed his great pleasure in hearing the news and told me I needed some time to learn the language. After several stories of his younger days, when a few of his former teammates ended up in Brown University's squad, he offered to let me stay with his family for free the next summer. The suggestion was too great to pass up, considering that I could simultaneously train for the next hockey season. He contacted the assistant coach at Brown and explained my situation and his reasoning for me to play another junior season. The university was willing to wait and follow my progress throughout. As a result, I was on my way to Edmonton after the completion of this hockey season.

The next summer in Edmonton, Bob, along with his wife, Joan, and their son, Patrick, treated me like their own family member. They provided room and board without asking anything in return. They bought me dictionaries, which I carried with me virtually everywhere I went. I began translating simple newspaper articles and explaining to Bob my understanding of them at random, one-on-one sessions. For some time, I had noticed Bob's skeptical responses toward my progress, for which I could not blame him at all. My English was nowhere close to the minimum required fluency and knowledge. I could not even hold a legitimate conversation, much less show competence in reading, writing, and comprehension. The goal seemed unattainable, but Bob and Joan never let me know their true thoughts. Only later, after many years together, did they admit that the task in front of me seemed too heavy to master. In the meantime, I focused on the present and did my best at accomplishing my goal. I dug my nose into books and newspaper articles, spending countless hours, with my dictionaries along my side. No way was I going to fail. My parents relied on my success to keep my sisters strong. They looked up to me and persevered in their own way. I decided that education would be my way into a better world and hockey would be the means of attaining that goal. I understood that success in hockey, be it professional or otherwise, would last only for some time and could end abruptly. But education would last for a lifetime. Therefore, with many uncertainties ahead of me, I committed my full efforts to improving my English.

That summer, several of the former Druzhba-78 players had gathered in Edmonton through their close friends and contacts. Some of them trained together. I, on the other hand, could not financially afford to sign myself up for the sessions and trained separately. All of us would hang out together and remember the "good" days with Ivan. We acted out some of his speeches and weird behaviors during Druzhba's after-practice meetings. We laughed about it and saw it in humorous ways. But no one ever spoke of the more personal experiences of Ivan's atrocious behavior. No one, except for the two boys who were with me during the judgment night in Uzhgorod, knew of the soccer "penalty kicks." No one knew about Ivan's visit to my home and his violent delivery of punches on my face and stomach. No one knew how after the captains' drawing, Ivan made me do squats naked in front of him and then violently struck my head in several places with his hockey stick. But we all knew that each of us had plenty of similar stories that transpired on an individual basis, outside anyone's knowledge. No one doubted his insanity and tyrannical mind-set, but settled that nothing could be done about it. Personally, I was simply glad to be away from him and hoped karma would be his ultimate judge. I believe that everything eventually comes full circle, and Ivan's judgment would come when he expected it the least. I believe he would die alone with no one beside his bed and nobody at his funeral. But at this moment, Ivan's life was the least of my worries, only my own. I had to survive. I had to prove myself worthy, regardless of all of Pravilov's claims of my pathetic existence. I was simply glad that someone was willing to help me, and they felt contrary to Ivan's words. They offered their support, and under any circumstances, I could not disappoint them. When my former Druzhba teammates found out about my plans to attend a university, some of them scoffed at my chances and encouraged me toward professional hockey in lower-level leagues. "You can still earn good money there," they would say. Seeing that I could not convince them otherwise, I simply responded that one more year of juniors would not hurt me a bit. If college did not work out, I would then pursue my professional career.

As the summer of 1998 went on, I continued my study of English. My dictionary had become my constant companion. Nothing could pass my attention and any article was a game. Simultaneously, I trained myself for the upcoming season in hopes that more universities would notice my performance. Bob helped me to find another junior team in Western Canada under the notion that being surrounded by the English-speaking population, my language skills would improve at a greater pace than in French-speaking Quebec. Thus, I ended up playing for the Powell River "Spruce Kings" in British Columbia. There, I exposed myself to even more scouts from several universities and became further encouraged about my goal. I bought myself a book about English writing and an SAT book that helped me to prepare for the test. In addition, I joined the city's high school, although after several days, I realized the pace was too fast and it would confuse me even further. So I quit. The rest of the season I spent studying English on my own, making tiny progress each week at a time.

The test drew closer and I gradually lost my confidence, believing my deficient English would undermine my goals. It was scheduled the second week of January, early in the morning. This was problematic as our team arrived from a road trip the night before and I could not review anything that I studied earlier. My teammates' discouragement did not help either. A few ridiculed the idea that I considered taking the test. "You cannot even hold a fluent conversation," they declared to me. I knew they were right, but I also knew that not everything turned out so bad. Throughout the hockey season, I used the SAT book to study the system of the test. I learned that for each incorrect response, one-third of a point would be taken off, whereas no points would be jeopardized if the response was left alone. In such circumstances, I decided to use my good knowledge of mathematics to answer every possible question and leave the English part virtually blank. This, I thought, was my only way out. During the test, I followed my plan exactly. With only few English questions answered, I focused my full energy on math. When completed, for one reason or another, I felt good about my chances. I contemplated that if the test was not passed, at least there was an excuse and I would pursue my professional career sooner. Otherwise, the result would be just another break in my favor.

When the good results came in a few weeks, I could not hold my excitement. But more importantly, I delivered the news to my Powell River teammates, who, in turn, were surprised that I actually pulled it off. To make the news even sweeter, two of the players, who critiqued my decision in taking the test, had failed, feeling embarrassed in front of the whole squad. However, I could not celebrate yet. By now, the end of the season approached and according to all interested universities, all full-ride positions that year had been filled, leaving me with only partial offers. Not being able to afford any of them, I could only wait and hope somebody would turn out. After the season and during the following summer, a few universities kept in touch, offering full or partial tuition without room and board, but I continuously refused. Then, I caught my break from an unexpected source. Toward the end of the summer, I joined one of the conditioning camps that Perry Pearn (then assistant coach of the Ottawa Senators) ran in Edmonton, Alberta. After one of my sessions on the ice, Bob randomly mentioned to him my situation, probably without any second thought that something would happen. To my good luck, Perry contacted Jacques Martin (then head coach of Ottawa Senators), who, in turn, knew Bill Wilkinson. He was recently hired as the head coach of the newly inaugurated Wayne State University D-1 hockey program located in Detroit, Michigan. Through this contact, Bill sent one of his assistant coaches, Danny Brooks, to look at me, the result of which was a full scholarship offer. Without any other similar offer on the table, I decided this was probably my only chance. By the third week of August, I saw no other prospects for full scholarship and, eventually, signed the letter of intent.

Although the hockey program was just initiated at Wayne State University, which meant time was needed to gain a widespread NCAA reputation, I saw some personal benefits in the undertaking. First, to refuse a free education would be very foolish of me. "Isn't this what I came here for?" I would ask myself repeatedly. Second, I understood that I would have a legitimate chance to become a starter and, perhaps, one of the leading players on the squad from the beginning. Third, I understood that Michigan was a great hockey environment and hoped that being in the midst of it would provide more exposure and a greater chance to make it to a professional level. To me, this was my second chance in hockey. But most of all, this was the opportunity for a postsecondary education that I would not have had a chance to pursue in Ukraine. I saw no downside.

Upon my arrival at Wayne State University, I soon found out that I was required to take a TOEFL (Test of English as a Foreign Language) exam, without which I could not enroll in any courses and be officially admitted into the school. Knowing the inadequate level of my English, I asked if this could be avoided. My efforts came to no avail. I took the test and soon received negative results. Accordingly, instead of enrolling myself in courses and practicing with the hockey team, I was placed in the ESL (English as a Second Language) section to improve my language skills. To say I was disappointed would be an understatement. Most of all, I could not afford the classes and notified Bob that I should probably think of another alternative. In response, he contacted the university administration and negotiated a deal where he would pay about half of my bill, and the rest would come the following year. He also covered my room and board for the entire semester, during which I was enrolled in the ESL program. I could not be more grateful to my friend for this gesture, continuing my determination in studies and training alike. So, the first semester, my duties were to improve my English in order to make myself eligible to take university courses and join the hockey team.

With Bob's financial assistance and with my studying efforts, I was able to improve my English skills dramatically. After a single semester, I had passed the test in every category but reading comprehension. There, I was required to read an article or a passage and answer a series of questions. My skills were not up to par yet, and I needed to take another English reading class in order to graduate from the ESL program. Because I was now eligible for full-time university courses, the ESL reading class presented an extra burden on my schedule. I decided not to focus on it and completely directed my full efforts at fulfilling the accredited university curriculum. Without finishing the ESL class with good marks, I could test out of it in the summer by simply taking another portion of the TOEFL exam. This could be done in Edmonton, and by that time, I expected my English skills to improve even greater. Therefore, there was no reason to overwhelm myself with an unnecessary load of schoolwork. The focus must be on the priority that kept hockey eligibility alive. The academic eligibility allowed me to join the hockey team on the ice, so by the second semester, the university provided me with an athletic scholarship that I needed so desperately. Actually, the head coach approached me with a proposition that I would not play the rest of the season but only practice, leaving the entire four following years of eligibility. This was an enticing alternative, but I opted out of it. I was not confident in my academic abilities based on English proficiency and thought that my road here would end sooner regardless; hopefully, with an offer from an NHL club. With this in mind, I declared I would begin playing immediately and forgo the optional year. As a result, the winter semester of 2000 became the starting point of my college hockey career.

The next summer, I arrived back in Edmonton, again taking quarters at the Bruce family's house. Again, the routine of training and improving my English resumed. Without a delay, I signed myself up for the reading and comprehension portion of the TOEFL exam. This would happen in July, but in the meantime, another good friend of mine (Walter Babiy) offered to let me help him on his farm about an hour away from the city. He was a former organizer of two of Druzhba's western Canadian tours and welcomed me with open arms. The calmness and peaceful environment of the farmland allowed me to ease my nerves and think deeply about my past and future. I thought about my priorities. Shortly after my arrival, I found out that he knew nothing about what transpired in his own house when Ivan and two other Druzhba boys stayed over. Walter explained that when one of the boys showed up with a cheek the size of a watermelon, Ivan's explanation was that both boys had gotten into a fight, and one of them had gotten the worst of it. I immediately explained that our former coach had evaded the truth, and that he was the culprit of the beat-up player. I gradually realized that Walter, like many other "outsiders," suspected some kind of wrongdoing on Ivan's part but could not prove his doubts. The information I told him opened his eyes about the true identity of Druzhba's coach.

At the time, Walter worked on his book, *Reign of Fear*, which told the story about the Druzhba hockey team and his experiences with it. Having another Druzhba player on his farm that summer, he was able to retrieve an abundance of new information. My former teammate and I would humor ourselves with Druzhba stories and exchange some of the brutal scenarios we witnessed. When Walter heard what happened to the boy who Ivan used instead of a punching bag in his own house, he immediately contacted the publisher to put the book on hold. Walter began randomly recording our stories as we told them and, each time, was shocked at how disturbing they were. He told us that he saw Ivan drink himself into oblivion and threatened the police. He explained about his suspicions while observing our quiet and motionless behavior in his presence. But this was another level. Our stories revealed a gruesome picture and he never thought this could be possible. Walter was also surprised that we were able to look at Ivan's humanitarian deficiencies with humor. To him, such atrocities were upsetting. When asked, we would say that this was the only way to be sane and continue moving on. At one point, I told my Druzhba teammate about the judgment night in Uzhgorod, after which we could not stop laughing. We assimilated Ivan's facial expressions and came up with different reasons for which I was punished. Noticing our laughter, to which he was already used to and knew what it meant, Walter inquired about the story. After hearing about my brutal encounter with Ivan, he stared at us in disbelief, missing any comedy in it. Regardless of his reaction, I told Walter he could put the story in his book and, if Ivan decided to challenge him, I would step in to support my claim. With time, Walter probably heard a few more stories from other Druzhba boys who were in Edmonton, but overall, not many wanted to share the experiences.

My time on the farm had ended in about six weeks. Although much of the work was not easy, I enjoyed the fresh air and had my former Druzhba teammate alongside for company. Walter even paid for my services, which I did not expect. Enjoying complementary room and board, as well as the peace and quiet, was enough and I felt asking for pay would be rude and out of place. But when offered, I could not refuse. I had a big loan on my shoulders that needed immediate attention and a big portion of the money would help this cause. The time I spent on the farm was plenty to recover from the hectic pace at the university, and with a fresh mind, I returned to Edmonton. There, I resumed training for the upcoming hockey season and, as usual, continued improving my English. In four weeks, I passed the TOEFL and relieved myself of the additional burden. From then on, I could entirely direct my attention at hockey and completing official university courses.

The next three years at Wayne State University had opened my eyes to many things. In the first year alone, I probably read more textbooks than I had done during all my high school years in Ukraine. When Druzhba-78 traveled three months at a time during the school season, we carried none of the assigned textbooks. All the traveling provided no incentive for studying, and most instructors in our high school worried more about the presents we brought back for them than anything else. After my initial two years at WSU, I had already decided on my major in business management but could not make up my mind on a minor. In one of the prerequisite classes (psychology 101), I had learned about the 1971 Stanford University prison experiment that was designed by Philip Zimbardo for two weeks but ended in six days due to sadism and abuse on the assigned prisoners. The scenario had a significant resemblance to what had transpired at many of Druzhba's team meetings. I instantly recalled the Elektrenay experience, where Ivan assigned one group of players to be fascists, creating instant resentment from the rest of the group. I remembered the Temnaya days, when Ivan provoked the entire team to perform beatings upon one player while the player's head was covered by a dark cloth. I could definitely not forget the Detroit scramble, whereupon he wished his players would turn against each other like a hungry pack of wolves. The only difference between the Stanford prison test and experiences on Druzhba was in the age of the participants, although no one, regardless of how old they are, should go through this. Relatively, events mentioned above would only constitute a small portion of what I had recalled. The humiliation and abuse never stopped from almost the first moment in 1986 to the final days. As a result, after some thinking, psychology became my choice. No matter how much I wanted to, the memories of Ivan's constant rage and abuse would not subside. I became interested in uncovering the motives behind the unforgivable cruelty he inflicted upon me and my teammates. The eventual revelation, I thought, would allow me to deal with my anger more easily and, perhaps, forgive the tyrant. I hoped to make peace with what happened and let the bastard be.

However, the more I read the angrier my emotions became. By my last year at the university, I began to feel the magnitude of my rage. During hockey games, I wanted to destroy my opponents, but more so, I wanted to inflict as much pain as possible to release the stress. I began to receive many penalties, and the penalty box had become a very frequent destination. One of the assistant coaches, I remember, jokingly would remind me before an important game the outcome of the boxing fight in the movie *Rocky 4*, saying that I should avenge my comrade. But what he did not understand was that I never lacked the motivation; only, it was in a different direction. Hockey became my outlet for emotional release. Toward the end of my four years at Wayne State, I also hoped that an NHL team would give me a chance to play at the highest level. If I made it, the plan was to use my influence to let the story out. Such an experience, I believed, should not be withheld from the public, especially when Ivan traveled around the world and promoted himself as a highly moral individual. He ran—and still continues to run—hockey clinics for children throughout North America and, by that time, also began receiving help from Gene Kenasevich's (former NHL player) funding contributions. Knowing where the money went during my time on Druzhba-78, I became suspicious that he kept it all, or at least most of it, for himself. To me, this was unacceptable and making the NHL became my next goal.

Walter's book, *Reign of Fear*, has helped to spread the facts about the cruelty of Ivan's coaching and teaching methods. As expected, Pravilov denied everything, calling everyone who provided some bits of information liars. Apparently, we all just conspired against him due to our inability to make it to the NHL. Some of the players who departed from Druzhba earlier in North America provided affidavits of Ivan's "unorthodox" behavior, to which his response was that they used the information as an excuse in order to stay. He further used my former Druzhba teammate's (who was and is one of the very few from Druzhba-78 who kept his loyalty to our former coach) influence in the NHL to deny the allegations. I could not believe that after so many years, the player continued to be brainwashed by the monster who relentlessly used his fists and brutal influence upon him. I could not believe that after so many years he could not realize that what happened was wrong by any interpretation.

People around North America would constantly ask me if the beatings and abuses by Ivan were true. I always responded yes without any hesitation. I would add that not many would understand the true horror, and explaining the details was pointless, unless someone had gone through a somewhat similar experience in their life. Some believed, but most looked at me with skepticism and cynicism. They were probably conflicted over how someone could do such things when many in North America raved about him. I would explain there were many signs of abuse that passersby saw but never paid much attention to. Everyone surrounding the team saw our complete silence in Ivan's presence. No one dared to make a sound out of fear of being reprimanded later, behind closed doors. There were also constant swellings of the boys' cheeks that Ivan easily passed off as a result of our fights among each other. In addition, our robotic behavior in his presence could not be mistaken for anything else but abuse, but people would always smile and say how well behaved and disciplined the boys were. In my interpretation, I would always say that discipline and abuse had a fine line, and to Ivan, such line did not exist. People would also ask me why then there was no proof, to which I also had a response. He was very smart about it and always kept "outsiders" away from knowing the truth. A player who joined our team on a temporary basis was never included in meetings where someone would be physically abused. A person traveling with our team was always kept at a distance when violence was included.

After completing my fourth year at WSU, I had gotten a tryout with the Edmonton Oilers, which was my only chance into the big league. It lasted about ten days and, eventually, the team let me go. My next option was to play in the lower divisions or travel across the ocean and play on a European team. This was a difficult decision to make; after all, I had some school left to complete my degree. Furthermore, I was a twenty-five-year-old undrafted player who did not make the NHL in his first try. My chances of accomplishing my goal were slim. The rest of my career could be spent scraping dollars together, trying to make ends meet, while losing precious time to finish my education. When priorities came into place, I opted out of professional hockey and pursued what I thought was best in the long run. To justify my decision further, I had an American girlfriend, who had lived her entire life in the Detroit suburbs. Playing hockey would require much traveling abroad. For her, it would mean leaving her life behind and following my way. I felt the hockey route would jeopardize our relationship and felt a strong conviction that my place was in Detroit, Michigan. Some thought I was crazy, leaving what I had worked for my entire life. I, on the other hand, felt at peace and had no regret. I believed this was my happy ending after so many years of struggle for survival and understanding. It was also my happy beginning that gave new perspective and light. I fell in love and could not compromise our separation. I felt balanced and no longer vengeful. It became my personal heaven. Shortly after, I contacted her with the news, explaining that I was ready to move to Detroit and make it my home. She happily accepted my arrival, and we never looked back ever since. Her entire family had opened their arms and welcomed me with love and joy. Their gradual affection made my heart melt and, with time, I saw no other way but to marry the girl of my dreams. After three years of dating, I proposed. She excitingly said yes, opening the door into a new chapter in our lives.

In the meantime, I had almost completed the university program, having two semesters to go. I continued my studies and began coaching and instructing small children in ice hockey. Coaching was an invaluable experience, because the longer I did so, the more I understood my true calling. Children responded well to my methods. I enjoyed instructing and coaching them, the way a teacher would. Upon the completion of the business management program at WSU and marrying, I concluded that teaching would be my future career. After a few probes in the working world, I went back to school for a teaching certification. WSU would graduate me only with a master's degree, which would eventually create many complications in the hiring process. So looking elsewhere, I had found a perfect fit at Eastern Michigan University (EMU), which offered post-baccalaureate certification. This was perfect because the school was within forty-five minutes of driving distance, and my resident tuition now cost me twice less than when I was under an international status. The decision was made, and in January of 2007, I enrolled at EMU to complete my teaching certification.

All along, I never stopped wondering about Ivan's motives behind his cruel treatments of his players. From the beginning, I suspected his demeanor to be a result of the Iron Curtain system of secrecy and fear. From the late 1920s, Josef Stalin created it in order to eliminate and exterminate his opposition, setting the groundwork for succeeding generations of Soviet citizens. The fear of punishment had engulfed the entire Soviet population. Robert Conquest in his *Stalin: Breaker of Nations* (1991) demonstrates the degree to which people were tormented. "Some results were as absurd as they were dreadful. At a provincial meeting there was an ovation when Stalin's name was mentioned, and no one dared to be the first one to sit down. When, finally, an old man who could stand no longer took his seat, his name was noted and he was arrested the next day." Very few dared to speak or even think otherwise, for there would always be cruel consequences. The system created an elaborate network of spies and informers, and no one, except Stalin himself (perhaps), possessed a complete immunity from persecution and extermination. A similar analogy could be applied in Ivan's case, where he created a system of fear and punishment on a smaller scale. We were interrogated for every unsatisfying move or spoken word. With time, I truly began believing that Ivan had his informers somewhere out there. Because of my father's random accusations about my "betrayal," and that I was a fascist, I assumed he was one of them without realizing so. Ivan liked him and used him against me. My mother, on the other hand, had confronted Ivan once, but instead of letting her know what he thought, his whole fury was unleashed on my shoulders. At that moment, my father would intervene, instructing her to leave the subject alone. "It is between our son and his coach," he said to her, "and you should keep your curious nose out of it." She could not fight both of them at once and backed away. I also believe that the players could not completely trust each other in this regard either. We kept our thoughts and beliefs to ourselves, not giving others a reason for a suspicion. The players who joined our team later, especially the ones toward the end, had noticed that Ivan would often ask players about any suspicious behavior. I later heard them say we were a group of "rats" and informers.

Although Ivan's decisions were based on his personal values and beliefs, he was also a product of a system that perpetuated the cycle of subjugation and abuse. He was undereducated and was self-taught in many aspects of his life. Without a wider base for his educational background, he believed that fear was the only solution to all problems. Children were no exception, and he treated us like he would treat anyone on this planet. He saw no wrong in constant humiliation and physical abuse. He took no second thought behind the discriminative remarks he used so often against us. The system taught him to be cruel and merciless, to never be open to alternatives. He was easily swayed to live in this manner without opening his eyes to any positive means of achieving his goals. As I learned later, it would always be easier to follow the crowd and succumb to the ways from the personal past, but only a few could open their eyes, learn, and accept the alternatives. Ivan was not one of them. He lived in an enclosed world, believing everyone was against him. The system made him the puppet of the Stalinist regime, and he used it to instill fear in whoever approached him. My mother became one of his victims and, after one confrontation, could not fight any longer.

Other parents had similar experiences. Some confronted Ivan with their accusations, and Ivan would use any means to manipulate their children. He would constantly ridicule them, as well as their parents, in front of the rest of the team during our after-practice meetings. He would brainwash our minds about proper ways to live. Also, every meeting would virtually always end with questions or comments that each of us was supposed to tell. Some of those comments informed Ivan of what a certain player did or did not do, which gave him an extra subject to ponder about or to decide the severity of the consequences.

One day, walking into a bookstore, I found an interesting account of a boy who was called "It." The author, Dave Pelzer, gave a vivid description of his torments in 1970s from his sadistic mother who turned her childhood anger and rage against her own son. I could closely relate to the accounts of his experiences, when he was forced to hold soap in his mouth and was locked in the bathroom with toxic fumes released at full. I could vividly see the scene in my mind when his mother would, without any warning, punch him and kick him in the stomach until he could no longer move. I could clearly relate to scenes of her constant threats and a desire to eliminate his self-esteem and the ability to fight back. His father closed his eyes at the events surrounding him and would always back away from confrontation with his unbalanced wife. He always found an excuse and would only mutter that the boy probably deserved what he got. Those same words came out of my father's mouth when I received a brutal punishment from my coach. I could not find refuge in anyone, so the purpose of my existence was constant personal survival. As I read the book, my blood boiled with anger. But I admired Dave's mental stamina and his ability to retain his sanity in the face of all obstacles. I could not fathom the enormous strength of his will, knowing that his heart did not become corrupted by hatred and feelings of vengeance. Love was the answer. Only love and goodwill could fight such monsters.

The story of survival and eventual revival of Dave Pelzer became my inspiration. Now I understand that regardless of the intentions of my adversary and his methods to take my self-esteem and self-concept away, I could still retain my humanity and move on in peace. All of a sudden, an epiphany hit me and now I faced a new world. This world was full of opportunities. From now on, instead of maintaining damage control, I saw the blessings in front of me. I had married the girl who loved and supported me since the day we met. She took me in her heart the way I was, regardless of my past. The burdens of my former life are behind me and I see a bright light into the future.

In two years, I completed the post-baccalaureate teaching certification at EMU. I had a clear view of my life in front of me and enjoyed thinking that I finally figured out who I was and what I wanted. I put enormous effort into accomplishing my academic goals, but even more so, I focused on dealing with my past. I confronted it and realized that nothing could change what happened before. The mistakes of my parents and wrongdoings of my former coach should not undermine the circumstances of my life. I should focus on my new family and make certain that history would not repeat itself. With that in mind, I began slowly forgiving my parents. I became convinced that their passive attitudes and inability to actively respond were also the result of long years of living in constant fear to object under the Soviet oppression. This made me conclude that Ivan was very smart after all. He realized what could be used against my parents and deployed it to induce his will upon me. He used fear and abuse to subdue my freewill and make me do and say, without realizing so, exactly what he wanted.

After such revelation, again, I began contemplating on the fact that I, regardless of the bad experiences, stuck around with Ivan for as long as I did. What motivated me to continue accepting the abuse, when I had a choice to flee and refuse on many occasions? Unlike earlier, this time I had a response. There was no motivation or desire. I resisted all along. But I also could not see any other way and thought this was the way grownups treated their children. Prior to Ivan, my father did not shy away from whipping my rear end with either a soldier's belt or a jump rope. He would use it in any occasion where he thought I was not obedient. When Ivan came along, I had received the punishments from both of them and simply did not know any other way. Thus, my goal became to survive the childhood years in order to call myself a man later. This mind-set disallowed me to openly resist and look at the situation from a different perspective. The passive attitude was my way to stand up for myself. I was not an individual, but a subdued citizen of the secretive and frightful system, and, as a result, made no efforts in objecting to the cruelty. Surviving any onslaught made me feel like a manly and worthy person. Any protest would be considered complaining and whining, which could be easily ridiculed and looked down upon. As Ivan sometimes preached, "Squeeze your teeth and move on without a sound." And so I did.

I also came to another conclusion. Over many years, Ivan was the target of my anger, but with time, I saw that he had nothing to do with it. He was a schmuck and a liar who deserved none of my personal attention. He was a tyrant and a child abuser who, one day, would get a taste of his own medicine without my involvement. He was an undereducated and ignorant individual who fell under the spell of the Soviet system of fear and punishment. He was oblivious to educating himself about positive means of achieving his goals, and I could not blame him for it. The sensation of power and control of everything and everyone that surrounded him was intoxicating. He abused his power and made everyone around him his subjects. Nevertheless, what bothered me were my own parents, especially my father. How could they, in their right mind, allow this sadistic monster to abuse their child? How could they look me in the eye and say they wished me the best childhood possible? How could they not believe the rebellious actions during the times of my escape from home? Would I ever be able to completely forgive them for their incompetence as my parents?

I love them both to death, but until my recent trip to Ukraine I could not discuss with them the true events of my secret past. I had waited for them to begin the conversation and apologize, thinking they might have known about the cruelties, but it had not happened. However, since my recent trip home, my trust for them has completely returned. I was able to talk about my past on Druzhba-78 and discuss the motives behind their former decisions. My parents truly saw no harm in pushing me back, disallowing me to quit. They never heard me complain or say anything that would be a good reason for my departure from the team. My mother explained that she took the blame upon herself for my escapes, and Pravilov was nowhere in the picture.

Today is more than a year after my graduation from EMU. I currently work as a teacher in a local school. I also continue instructing and coaching young children in ice hockey. My family surrounds me and helps me adjust to new circumstances. I have great friends who made this day possible, and their warmth and goodwill will never be forgotten. I have friends who I consider my close family, with whom I feel comfortable talking about the cruel past. With them, I have seen the true loving side of the spectrum. I am happy to have what I have. But is the achievement worth the means that I was exposed to? On the one hand, I feel grateful for my childhood experience. I would not be as strong as I am now. I would not appreciate the good nature of people as much as I do now. I would not have met my wife and her family, and I would never have the pleasure of knowing many good friends who came along on my way. But on the other hand, I would never wish anyone to become the victim of similar circumstances and be forced into an unimaginable malice. The question above would be the ultimate revelation for me, but I rather take my time and let it show me the answer. I have reached the point where I could leave my past behind and let the future be the guide. Now, I am in control of my destiny. I make the decisions that lead my future path.

Final Note

Some might ask, "How has your life been affected by the years you spent with Ivan Pravilov?" For many years, my soul felt unfulfilled. My heart was constantly in search of a seemingly invisible goal. Something was devouring me from within, and I could not understand what. Unexpectedly, time and experience pushed me to recognize that void. Since my experiences as a member of Druzhba-78 with Ivan, I needed a way to release the negative and bring in the positive. I constantly searched for approval in all aspects of my life. My struggles after Druzhba could have further destroyed my self-esteem. I could easily have become psychologically unstable and blamed it on the abuse rendered by my former coach. I could be miserable day in and day out, horribly unpleasant around anyone in close proximity. The easiest choice would be to give in to my emotions and live in perpetual self-pity. The temptation was great. However, I refused to do so. I could not bear anyone's pity toward my dark past. I would not force my burden upon my friends and family. My decision was to fight the built-up anger and become an individual with values of my own. I strived to rise above my unpleasant past. I wanted to view my experiences in a positive way, where uncertainties and hardships brought out the best in me. It would make me spiritually stronger and more self-reliant.

Initially, the anger devoured me from the inside out, continuing the destructive path that Ivan laid for my future. It gave me no rational perspective on what I personally considered important and valuable. Only a peaceful mind and understanding of who and what I was brought a sense of fulfillment and accomplishment. I filled the void by recognizing that I was my own person and that no one else should control the outcome of my life. Knowing myself, I could leave the past behind and look forward to new, future challenges. With full pride and elation, I could say, "I am who I am, and not what Ivan had in mind for me. I can think for myself, instead of what was 'instructed.' I can make my own decisions and plan my own life."

After the separation from Ivan at eighteen and for many years to come, I was consumed by the idea of forgetting the unpleasant experiences. The years had gone by, but the memories continued resurfacing. They came more and more frequently, holding me back from setting my life in order. The anger within me rose, perpetuating the feeling of hopelessness. I felt trapped in my own skin, believing nothing good would result from such emotions. Every time this happened, though, I thought of my friends and the amount of help they provided to keep me going. I thought of Bob Bruce and Walter Babiy, whose unwavering support inspired me to stay on course and to make the best of what was given. Observing others' life experiences helped me understand the virtue of my situation. Trying to suppress my memories would not allow me to move forward. They would haunt and pursue me wherever I went. My course of action, therefore, was to confront the demons of my past. There would not be any sorrow for what happened. There would not be any feelings of regret for former experiences. There would also be no anger and rage toward the individual who caused me the unbearable pain. This resolution, eventually, became my means of releasing the negative and bringing in the positive. It was the salvation to my damaged soul.

My life continues as a work in progress. It starts to take its course, and I am finally beginning to see the fruits of my labor. Dealing with my mental state and emotional balance is what I consider to be the greatest challenge. By overcoming, not forgetting, the past and focusing my energy on the future, each day has brought me closer to a resolution. I finally came to a better understanding of the circumstances under which my former Uzhgorod "masters" treated me to satisfy their boredom and entertainment. Philip Zimbardo's book, *The Lucifer Effect*, has taught me how systemic influence could foster a good person's evil behavior toward others. It brought me closer to understanding that Ivan, not my teammates, had created the atmosphere of fear, intimidation, punishment, terror, dehumanization, humiliation, etc. I hold no grudge toward them and only hope they now understand and realize the negative effects of their former behavior.

With time, I also recognized that Ivan was not the primary focus of my anger, my own parents were. How, after all, could they allow Ivan to abuse their own child the way he did? How could they not see the obvious signs of my vulnerability? After this revelation, I felt lighter on my feet, figuring that my parents would be easier to deal with, but I spoke too soon. Not until recently had I revealed their motives. Up to that moment my mind was filled with many uncertainties. What if they knew what Ivan did to me and simply closed their eyes? What if their unresponsive behavior was purposeful after all? This could have been another punch below the belt and several more years would pass before I could make peace with it. From one perspective, my goal was to face the problem and ask the straight question, but my subconscious delayed the moment because I love them dearly. I understood that circumstances might have forced their beliefs, but as my parents, their sole duty was to protect and defend their child. This could have been another betrayal on their part that I would not have taken lightly. All those years I waited for their explanation, and it finally arrived. My parents had only good intentions. They did not, as I speculated all along, know of Ivan's horrible deeds and sadistic methods. It seems too good to be true, but the story does have a really good ending. My mind is clear. Life goes on. My past is not troublesome anymore. The only aspect of my past I could take with me in the future is the fact that I have become much stronger and significantly self-assured individual.

From a psychological perspective, I realized that such a story could be difficult to emotionally comprehend for those who neither experienced nor witnessed such abuse. If you have children, imagine that such a fate had fallen on their shoulders. Imagine if nephews or nieces or other relatives who you love so dearly became victims of the mental and physical torments that Ivan had put all of "his" children through. Imagine your child/relative is beaten to the point where their anger reaches boundless proportions. Picture your child/relative being humiliated to a degree at which suicide seems to be the best solution and self-esteem could not drop any lower. Visualize your child/relative being constantly brainwashed that his/her parents are not qualified to care for them. According to Ivan, all they provided was actual birth, but nothing else that helped their children's upbringing. I wonder what reaction and response on your part would follow this revelation. What would be your emotional state then? How would these circumstances affect your attitude toward an individual like Ivan Pravilov? By imagining these scenarios, only then could you begin to understand the magnitude of this story.

The answer to the question about our attitudes toward individuals like Ivan Pravilov seems to be self-explanatory. What we really should be asking is why this monster continues to instruct and coach young children throughout North America and abroad. Why is he allowed in any proximity to any children? Why does this fugitive walk free, continuing to profit from the tyrannical empire he built with Druzhba-78? Why do the International Ice Hockey Federation (IIHF) and other national associations look past his record and allow him to believe he is invincible? Ivan's deeds are despicable. His demeanor and excuses are unacceptable by any standards of human nature. The least we can do is not allow him any further association with children. If you ask me, he should be locked up for the remainder of his natural life.